To my beloved mother Janette
and my beautiful wee sister, Vicky

Chapter One

Downing their shovels, the police search team bowed their heads in silence as the wreaths were placed next to the children's sandpit that covered the grave of a girl who had been missing for nearly seventeen years.

Two detectives laid the floral tributes on behalf of the girl's father and her sister. Both had attached notes with their own thoughts. Every detail of Vicky Hamilton's short life and gruesome death would now become public knowledge as the scale of the crime unfolded ...

But yesterday their words to her remained private.

Daily Mail, *14 November 2007*

*

CALL IT A sister's intuition, or maybe I had just become an expert on police protocol, but when I heard the familiar voice of CID officer Pat Gaughan on the other end of the telephone I had an overwhelming feeling that my 17-year search for my missing sister was about to end. Wednesday 14 November 2007 was a typical morning in our house, the little haven in Scotland I share with my partner Brian, our son John and my daughter Emma-Jane, and I was busying myself with the usual mundane pieces of housework.

Another day with my family. Another day, just like every other over the previous 17 years, when I wake up and the first thing I think about is my sister Vicky. Always there in my head, the haunting image of a young girl lost.

Now, almost two decades on, I was about to find the truth about her disappearance.

The call from Pat was out of character. I could tell that something was different. There was no usual friendly chat. And with just seven little words, he turned my world upside down. 'Are you going to be home later?'

I caught my breath. When a police officer asks you if you are going to be home, it can only mean one thing: he has something significant to tell you. Important news doesn't come in a phone call. It comes face to face.

My voice was reduced to a whisper as I replied: 'Yes. I'll be home.'

I came off the phone and sat motionless, going over Pat's words in my head. My emotions went into overdrive, my stomach was churning. Must keep busy. Must keep occupied. Why does he want me home? What is he going to tell me?

Deep down I already knew the answer.

Around an hour later, I jumped as the phone rang

again. It was Pat. Two of his colleagues were on their way to my house to speak to me. I didn't hear anything else he said. This was it. Face to face…

I called my brother and sister, twins Lee and Lindsay, to tell them to come home as soon as possible. Lee arrived within ten minutes. I met him in the hallway, threw my arms around him and gave him a big hug. He looked petrified, and there were tears in his eyes.

By the time Lindsay got my voicemail it was almost midday. She called me back as I had stepped into the back garden to get some fresh air and try and clear my head. I couldn't bring myself to tell her my suspicions over the phone, so I told her I'd send Brian to pick her up as soon as he could. As I finished the call I could hear Brian greeting the police officers at the front door.

I walked from the kitchen to the living room where the two officers were standing. When they saw me, their gaze, as if synchronised, dropped to the floor. The police are trained to impart bad news, but I suppose it is difficult to disguise body language in situations like this. I motioned to them to sit down, and they both sat on the same couch. Brian offered them coffee, but they politely refused. I went to our other sofa, facing them. Lee looked ashen-faced as he sat down next to me.

The atmosphere was tense, and I felt nauseous. Vicky had disappeared on the night of 10 February 1991, and after nearly 17 years of speaking to dozens of police officers about various aspects of Vicky's case, I couldn't believe I had arrived at this moment. All the years of campaigning. Hoping. Waiting. Praying. It had all come down to now. Although they had hardly said a word between them, I knew in my heart what these two police officers had come to tell me. I braced myself.

The female officer looked straight at me and said: 'You know we found a body at a house in Kent?' I nodded slowly, gripping the arm of the couch for support. She continued: 'We did some checks, and judging by the dental records, the body is Vicky's. I'm sorry.'

It's Vicky.

My God. It's Vicky. These were the words I'd waited almost 17 years to hear. They've found Vicky. I'd often wondered how I would react on hearing these words. I'd played it over and over in my head. It was bad news, but in a strange way, good news too, as Vicky had finally been found. It was the moment I had both yearned for and dreaded.

I was shaking and crying at the same time and Brian tried to comfort me. The room seemed to echo with voices. I got up off the couch and staggered through the kitchen and out the back of the house into the garden. I let out a scream: 'Noooo.' Then Brian was beside me and I fell into his arms, sobbing.

As I hugged him tightly I heard him, over my shoulder,

ask the police officers: 'Are you sure it is Vicky?' I understood why he asked it. There could be no mistakes. We had to be certain. The male officer replied: 'One hundred per cent sure. Sorry.' I heard Lee gasp and saw his hand move to his mouth in shock.

Vicky was dead. It was official. Our darling Vicky had been brutally murdered.

To think of my beautiful Vicky lying alone, buried in a garden at the other end of the country, just crushed me. In a strange way, I think the fact that her body was found 400 miles away from home, so far from her family, made it seem worse. On her own for nearly 17 years.

The police said she had been found with some of my mother's jewellery beside her body. She had borrowed some pieces from Mum when she came to visit me the weekend she disappeared – a bracelet and a couple of rings. Murdered while wearing her mother's jewellery. A young girl trying to be grown-up; a child on the cusp of adulthood. Taken from the streets by a serial sex killer.

That Wednesday our search had come to an end. My sister had been found. My sister was dead.

After the two police officers had broken the news of Vicky's death I sat in my tiny living room trying to take in the enormity of what I had just heard. Moments before they had arrived, I'd been watching live news bulletins from Kent. Two days earlier a police force had started digging up the garden of a house once occupied by Peter Tobin, a convicted murderer and sex offender. A man who at the time of Vicky's disappearance had rented a house in Bathgate, West Lothian, near where she was last seen. Reports had begun to come through on the news that police may have found a girl's body in the garden. But never once was my sister's name mentioned. Now the news programmes would be full of Vicky's name. Her picture. Her shallow grave. Her story.

At some point amid the chaos Brian left to pick up Lindsay, and when she arrived at the house, she was crying her eyes out. Brian had told her the bad news in the car. I always thought Lindsay was tough, almost resilient to the many problems the family had had over the years. But that day I saw her as a vulnerable child. She just crumbled. All I could do was hug her. Her big sister was dead. The girl she'd been robbed of growing up with. It was so difficult to find the words to say to her – something, anything to give her some comfort. Especially when my own heart had just been broken.

To hear that someone you love dearly – your own flesh and blood – has been killed is just too much for a human being to have to bear.

As the two police officers were preparing to leave, their apologies for bringing us bad news stirred me from my thoughts. As Brian accompanied them out of the living room and to the front door, I suddenly thought about my father – the man I hadn't spoken to for over two years. The man I call Michael because I can't bring myself to call him Dad. How would he take the news? He is so unpredictable it was hard for me to know how he would react.

The officers said they were on their way to tell him, but they had wanted to speak to me first. I asked them to pass on a message to my dad that if he wanted to call me he could. It was my olive branch to him, and I hoped he would grasp it.

I was beginning to think more rationally now after the initial shock and I thanked the officers for finding Vicky and breaking the news to us. I thanked them for all their hard work over the years. I was also sorry for them having to go and tell my father.

I called two of my closest friends, Gayle a former work colleague, and Angela, my oldest friend. Angela had grown up with me and, she in particular, had supported me every step of the way during the campaign to try and find Vicky. She was devastated when I told her the news, but between her sobs I could hear her making arrangements to leave her work in Glasgow and drive to Falkirk to be with me. I felt blessed to have such a dear friend.

It didn't take long for it to be all over the news: 'Vicky Hamilton's body found after 17 years,' the headlines screamed. I sat down. I couldn't believe this was happening. It simply didn't seem real. But it was true, and this was reality…

God only knows what fate befell Vicky. I didn't want to imagine what she went through. It's just too painful.

I knew that I would have to be strong for my family, especially Lee and Lindsay. They needed me more than ever now.

Soon relatives and friends started to arrive at the house, and the living room suddenly began to fill up. We watched the news over and over again. The noise of the television, the chatter of voices, all blended into the background. I was alone with my thoughts, and inside my head was a perfect calmness.

I walked outside. I breathed in the sharp, damp air. I looked up into the heavens. It was a beautiful evening and the stars were so bright as they lit up the night sky. I closed my eyes and imagined Vicky as I had known her – laughing, joking, full of life. I prayed for her. I prayed that she was with our mum and that she was happy now that at last she had been found after so long.

'I miss you so much, Vicky,' I said. 'I know you can hear me.'

I tried to banish the horrific thought of Vicky lying in that shallow grave. Instead I imagined her sleeping peacefully like a baby. Like the times as children we shared a bed, and I would watch her fall asleep first.

I used to look at her and smile. All warm and cosy under the covers. As she gave into sleep, she had the look of an angel …

Chapter Two

IT IS MY earliest memory; my first recollection as a child. I was barely four years old and winter had given way to spring. It was the day my little sister was born.

Vicky Faye Hamilton came kicking and screaming into the world just after 2.30 p.m. on 24 April 1975. A healthy baby weighing six pounds, nine ounces. It was a day that marked the beginning of a wonderful friendship.

Vicky was born in Falkirk Royal Infirmary, about five miles from our home, and I vividly remember running along the hospital corridor, rushing to get to the ward to see Mum – and my brand new sister.

Dad shouted at me to stop, and we stood together – father and daughter – in front of the two great big pale blue wooden doors with small windows on the top, at the entrance to the maternity ward. Dad bent down and grabbed me around the waist, hoisting me high so my nose pressed against the window; my breath steaming up the glass as he held me. I peered through. Mum saw me and waved. Alongside her bed was a small perspex cot.

My dad pushed open the ward doors and put me down. My feet slipped and slithered on the polished floor as I ran full pelt over to Mum's bed.

Dad walked straight to the cot and slowly reached in, gently picking up the tiny bundle wrapped in swaddling blankets. I instinctively stood on my tiptoes to get a better look. And there she was. My little sister. All wrinkly and pink with tufts of dark brown hair. She looked beautiful, like a little porcelain doll.

'Sharon, your sister is very special. You must help your mum look after her,' Dad whispered softly in my ear as I gazed in wonder at the tiny baby before me.

'I will, Dad. I'll look after her for ever,' I replied.

It is heartbreaking now when I take out photograph albums and look at pictures of my little sister as a baby, her bright eyes shining and her so-cute smile. Images of innocence. She was not to know that she would never be given the chance to grow up. She was not to know I would break my promise to her. Even big sisters can't protect you from everything.

*

It could never be described as love's young dream, but my parents' romance was nothing if it wasn't passionate – and whirlwind.

Jeanette Buszka and Michael Hamilton both worked

for Alexander's bus company in Falkirk. It was 1968. The Beatles topped the charts and winkle-pickers and drain-pipes were in fashion. They were both bus conductors, or 'clippies', as we call them in Scotland. Mum was a stunning-looking teenager, fresh-faced and attractive, and was regularly chatted up by passengers on her route. She was flattered by the attention they paid her.

She lived near Whitecross in Stirlingshire, a gritty down-to-earth village between Edinburgh and Falkirk, known rather unfortunately for its local brickworks – one of the biggest employers in the area. She was just 18 when she met Michael and she still lived with her mum Euphemia and younger brother David, her older brothers and sisters having married and moved away from the family home.

Before they got together both Mum and Dad were in serious relationships; Mum engaged to a young local man who also worked on the buses, and Dad had been dating a girl from the nearby Alloa area. He broke off the relation-ship as soon as he met Mum. I suppose you could call it love at first sight.

My dad had – and still has – a huge personality, and I think Mum just found it too hard to resist. He was out-going, loud and loved being the centre of attention. He seemed to always find the right words to say in any situa-tion, and Mum found him utterly charming.

Before long Mum broke off her engagement and took up with Dad. They were inseparable. She hung on Dad's every word, every turn of phrase. He had a hold over her, and at the time, she loved the feeling of security he brought to her life.

My father lived in Redding, a small village on the outskirts of Falkirk. He was the second oldest of five children. His elder sister Joy had married and moved out of the family home by the time he and Mum started dating, so he lived with his younger sister Gwen and his brothers John, Eric and Peter, who was just a baby. They lived with their mother in a small end-terrace house with four bedrooms.

Redding was – and still is – a close-knit community. It's the sort of place where everybody knows your personal business. But the upside is that when there is a crisis affecting your family, the villagers rally round and offer help and support by the bucketload.

It was a great place to bring up children, and there was a large grassy park behind my dad's house with a well-used playground.

As it turned out, their neighbours were a lovely couple who had a daughter called Christine. She would grow up to be a close friend of my mother's and a regular and much-loved babysitter for me and Vicky. She would also be instrumental in changing all our lives.

Mum and Dad's relationship blossomed quickly. They

were besotted with each other, and less than two years after they met, Dad proposed. Mum accepted immediately. The wedding date was set for 18 July 1970. But, no sooner had they told family and friends of their decision, than their plans were dealt a huge setback. My grandmother Euphemia caught a bad dose of the flu, and because she was terrified of going to the doctor, she ignored her symptoms until it was too late and she had developed pneumonia. Mum wanted to postpone the wedding, but surprisingly Gran insisted it should go ahead as planned. Mum always said that Gran didn't particularly like Dad, or feel he was good enough for her daughter. I suppose she went along with the wedding because she could see, despite her reservations, that Dad made Mum happy, and her daughter was very much in love.

Between her job on the buses, frenetic wedding plans and visiting Gran in hospital, the pressures took their toll on Mum, and she herself began to feel increasingly unwell. She had no appetite or strength, and the simplest of tasks seemed daunting. She was so exhausted one day my dad persuaded her to go and see the doctor for some tests – no mean feat as Mum had the same pathological fear of the medical world as my gran.

Just a week before the wedding, things took a turn for the better, and doctors gave Gran permission to leave the hospital to attend the ceremony. So, on a brilliantly sunny

July day, Mum and Dad were married in Mum's home church in Muiravonside. They were delighted that Gran made it to the church – although she was still very ill and due to return to hospital the next day. My dad's brother John was the best man and Mum's cousin Marlyn Beglin was chief bridesmaid. Mum was radiant. She was always proud of her long legs, so she, rather bravely, opted for a white lace mini wedding dress. I look at faded photographs of that day, and I think she looked amazing, with her dark brown hair piled fashionably high on her head. Dad and Uncle John looked dashing and handsome in their black morning suits. After the service, and photographs outside the church, the wedding party headed off to a nearby hotel for the reception.

They were the perfect couple. Handsome. Happy. So much in love.

Gran was too weak to cope with the reception, but Mum was just delighted that she was able to take part in her big day. Mum and Dad later ferried some of their guests to Gran's house for a nightcap. A perfect end to a perfect day.

Against the odds, Gran made a remarkable and un-expected recovery, and just a few weeks after the wedding was discharged and allowed to return to the family home in Whitecross. Mum and Dad decided to move in with her, allowing them to help her recover. It perhaps wasn't the ideal start to married life, but Mum's family needed her, and Dad understood.

*

'Congratulations Mrs Hamilton. You're pregnant,' the doctor proclaimed when Mum went back to the doctor's for the results of her tests. It was the last thing Mum expected. She was in shock, but ecstatically happy at the same time as she left the surgery. She wondered how Dad would take the news. They had talked about having children as most couples do, but they both anticipated parenthood a few years down the line. It wasn't something they had planned so soon, especially as they had only been together as a couple for a relatively short time.

Mum told me that when Dad heard the news, he said he was the luckiest man alive. He scooped her up in his arms and hugged her tightly. 'Perfect. Just perfect,' he said.

After the wedding, Mum and Dad went back to work while Mum's sister Helen helped care for Gran during the day. Then, suddenly, almost as quickly as she had recovered, Gran suffered a relapse and was rushed back into hospital. It was a terrible time for everyone. One day Mum went to visit, and when she arrived she was told that Gran had been moved to a private part of the ward. I'm sure that when she heard this she realised the outlook was grim. As she approached Gran's room she heard her scream in agony.

On 17 October 1970, Gran's pain ended and she passed away. She was only 50. My mother was still six months pregnant with me so I would never meet my grandmother.

After the funeral, Mum and Dad were homeless, until Margaret, my dad's mother, invited them to live with her. Her house was tiny and cramped. When I arrived in the world the following January, they decided it was time to get a place of their own. It came in the shape of a caravan on a site between Redding and Muiravonside. We were there for just a few short months until the land was sold off to make way for housing. I was around 12 months old when Mum and Dad applied to Falkirk Council for a house, and were lucky enough to be offered one in Redding. It was a three-bedroomed end of terrace at 58 Woodburn Avenue – the same street as my Gran Hamilton. The house had big bedrooms and a large garden at the front and the back of the house. This was to be our first real family home. Nothing could break this secure Hamilton family bond.

*

After Vicky was born I was so happy. I had a little sister. I can't recall a great deal about her as a baby. I thought she was just a little doll that Mum and Dad had got for me to play with, and I have early recollections of 'helping' mum change her nappies and bathe her.

According to Mum, as Vicky got older and was able to crawl, we both got into more scrapes and trouble than she ever thought possible. Being the older sister had its definite perks. When we were discovered doing something naughty, I would simply blame Vicky – and usually I got away with it. But being the older sibling also had its downside, and, just like in any family, I was sometimes forced to let her play with me when my friends came round to visit – not exactly good for my street cred.

We shared a bedroom and had bunk beds. Naturally I slept on the top, and Vicky was underneath. The room was filled to the brim with toys, and, typical girls, we both loved to play with dolls. Whether it was baby dolls or dress-up dolls, we loved them all and couldn't get enough of them.

Whenever we got dress-up dolls, Vicky, having brown hair, would get a brunette doll, and me a blonde one. We would often play for hours on end until it was bedtime, or until we fell out and ended up screaming at each other. Vicky may have been four years younger than me, but she could stand her ground. She was a tough little cookie, and I saw that trait in her develop as we grew up together.

One of my fondest memories was when Vicky was around fourteen months old. Dad took us to the local pet shop to pick out a dog to take home. Vicky and I loved animals, and the dogs we saw were cross-breeds with white and brown patches. I screamed in delight when we picked a particularly energetic puppy out from the litter.

'What shall we call him?' Dad asked. I said we should call him Patch, even though it was the name of our last dog. But the name fitted so perfectly.

When we left the pet shop, we took Patch to a nearby church where there was a grassy area to the back. I remember that day as if it was yesterday. I chased Patch around the churchyard, in and out of the bushes, while Vicky toddled behind squealing with delight.

*

Our childhood was happy, and we were a settled family unit. Although there was never a great deal of extra money around, Vicky and I never had to do without. There was always food on the table, and money for clothes when we needed them.

Dad was a real grafter, often working six days a week to provide for us. For years he worked as a delivery driver for a local potato merchants, known in the area as Tattie Wilson's. I remember his huge blue wagon, filled to the brim with fresh fruit and vegetables. Sometimes he would allow me to go with him on his rounds, and I used to watch wide-eyed in amazement and wonder at my big strong dad lifting big sacks of potatoes from his wagon and carrying them on his shoulder into the local shops around the Falkirk area. I loved 'helping' him. Vicky was still too young to come along, so it was just me and my dad. Our time. I would sit up front in the lorry with him watching the world go by in my 'high-up' position. Proud as punch and king of the road.

I felt very special, and when we stopped at the shops with deliveries, I would often get sweets from the owners for being a good girl and helping my dad. It was a great fun day out and I felt grown-up working with Dad. I always went home with lots of goodies, and I would – often reluctantly – share my spoils with my little sister.

My dad is an outgoing man who can make friends easily. Everyone in Redding knew him and a walk in the village with him would mean people continuously stopping him in the street to catch up on gossip. Redding was where his roots were, and where most of his family lived. There always seemed to be some aunt or uncle popping into the house for tea and a chat when I was growing up.

Mum was the homemaker, renowned for being practical. She was a natural, bringing up two children and juggling the pressures of domestic life while making the weekly wage stretch. In her spare time – not that she had much of it – she could be found in her chair in the living room either knitting or engrossed in some form of intricate needlework.

But it was her home baking that Vicky and I loved, and something I still miss to this day. The kitchen would fill up with the familiar aroma of scones toasting in the oven. Sometimes she would make one of our favourites – traditional Scottish tablet, a sugary fudge-like toffee, or fairy cakes.

If she was in the mood she would let us help her, and, once we had 'assisted', Vicky and I would fight over the remains of the cake mixture stuck to the sides of the baking bowl. We both always ended up a sticky mess with the sugary remnants around our cheeks and plastered through our hair. Then we would sit eagerly in front of the oven, impatiently waiting for our 'masterpieces' to cook. Later, as we tucked into the food, Mum would say without fail: 'Remember to leave some for Dad.' But more often than not we ended up scoffing the lot.

Vicky and I had a favourite game we played when Mum was busy and Dad was out working. We would make sure the coast was clear and select four of Dad's treasured LPs from the record rack, carefully taking out the black vinyl discs before putting them to one side. We would then take off our shoes and socks, and with our sticky feet, stand on the album covers and use them as makeshift skates. It was brilliant fun sliding up and down the living room carpet, although I would invariably have to signal to Vicky to stop giggling in case Mum caught wind of what we were doing. We became experts at this game, until inevitably Mum caught us mid-pirouette. She was livid, but of course I got the brunt of the row because I was older and should have known better. Vicky just smiled her innocent smile before we were both sent to our room to think about what we had done to Dad's prized record collection.

Mum was a pussycat with a loud miaow, and we knew exactly how to work her and wrap her around our little fingers. Luckily she never told Dad about our little game. Though we loved him, we didn't like to cross our father; we didn't like the feeling of his big hand slapping our backside when we were naughty.

I've been told by relatives that we were good, well-behaved children with impeccable manners. I suppose it was testament to just how happy and settled Mum and Dad were at the time. They were able to channel a great deal of time and attention into bringing us up. Luckily we got a solid grounding in manners and respect for our elders.

*

The silliest things pop into your head when you begin reminiscing about moments from your childhood. Our walk to school is one such moment. We lived about 15 minutes' stroll from the school and the 'proper' road would take Vicky and me down the 'fairy steps' – about 150 lopsided steps that led from Uncle John's house at the playpark, down through the woods and out to the school gates. Often at weekends Vicky and I would play in this small, charming wooded area, but on school days we would regularly take a shortcut through the 'Cow's Park'. This was a much quicker route home, and saved us valuable time as we rushed to get to our house for tea. The downside was that many a time we arrived home, dashing into the house with our shoes caked with cow dung – hence the name of the park.

Mum would be livid, scolding us as she caught a whiff of the two of us as we ran past her. Many times she banned us from walking that way home, and we always promised to stop – until the next time! It still makes me laugh, but it drove Mum to distraction.

Woodburn Avenue was a fantastic street to grow up in. It was a typical street in a working-class village, with a mixture of affluent families and households who obviously struggled financially. At various times my family belonged in both categories.

As children growing up in Redding, we had everything we could have wished for right on our doorstep. In the summer we would play outside, and we were kings of the big old oak tree about 50 yards from our front door. From one of the tree's huge branches hung our Tarzan swing, and children from the streets all around would converge here to take turns swinging from the giant bough.

There was also the 'loch' at the back of our house. Strangely, although it was called the loch, it wasn't filled with water – it was grass. I'm not sure of the origins of the place's nickname. Perhaps it was a waterway in the past and was filled in, but when Vicky and I were growing up, it was where we learned to ride our bikes. I suppose it was the Scottish equivalent of the village green – although, admittedly, not quite so picturesque.

People gathered there for all kinds of events. In the late autumn the children collected lumps of wood, old papers and bits of junk in a huge pile in preparation for bonfire night. This was always a big event in the village calendar, and most of the community would turn out and we watched excitedly as the adults set our mammoth bonfire alight. In the winter the 'loch' would become our own personal ski slope, and we all took turns at sledging down the hill past that old oak tree.

The 'loch' also had a small play area with three sets of swings and a roundabout. Vicky and I would take turns at pushing each other. It was a fantastic, safe place. A sort of nursery without walls. We knew every child in the village, and you were never short of a playmate.

All the houses around our way looked the same. I

always thought they looked like they had sad faces; they were a bit ramshackle and tired. Even so, I loved our home. It was secure and warm, especially when Mum lit our upstairs fire and the shadows danced on our bedroom walls. On these nights it seemed the house and everyone in it cosied up as one.

I also treasured it when it was full of friends. Mum and Dad were very sociable people and loved a good party. There were many nights when Vicky and I would be lying in our beds, and we would hear a deep bass sound reverberating through the living room ceiling and into our bedroom above. We loved these party nights. Often, if we could pluck up the courage, we would climb out of bed, creep down the stairs and huddle together at the bottom trying to peer through the living room's glass door to try and catch a glimpse of what was going on. We would see the shadows of people dancing and singing, their drink-fuelled noisy chatter filling the air. If the door was ajar we would possibly spot Mum in the kitchen, red-faced and fussily making snacks for her guests.

Sometimes, if we were spotted, we got sent straight back upstairs to bed, but occasionally Mum or Dad motioned us in to join in the party. Then Vicky and I instantly became the stars of the show and took requests to dance and sing. Mum and Dad never knew it, but often Vicky and I would secretly rehearse routines in our room in preparation for just such an occasion. We both loved showing off. Dad would put on one of his favourite songs, almost invariably Queen's 'Don't Stop Me Now' and that would be the cue for Vicky and me to take our routine to the 'stage'. By the time we finished our ears would ring with our captive audience's applause.

At the time it was the best feeling in the world, and Vicky and I would stand there with big beaming grins, milking every single second of it. Then everyone was on the floor dancing, and Vicky and I would join in.

*

When I was about six I asked why Dad didn't drive Tattie Wilson's potato van any more. Mum's eyes dropped and she said that he had sworn at his boss and he'd lost his job because of it. I remember thinking that it seemed a harsh punishment for simply swearing. Something didn't seem right, and there was a terrible atmosphere in the house. There were hushed conversations between Mum and Dad, and they immediately stopped what they were saying if I walked into the room.

I missed our trips in the big blue potato lorry. I also on some level knew that this meant we as a family would have less money, but I knew Dad would do whatever he had to do to support Mum, Vicky and me. For months we had little or no money coming in, and Mum performed miracles trying to make ends meet and stretch the small budget. Mum and Dad were both under a great deal of stress.

A lot of their so-called friends didn't hang around any more. And the parties stopped.

Mum was the worrier in the family, and it must have been a particularly tough time for her. Dad was more of an optimist. I suppose they balanced each other out. I would hear him reassuring her that their hard times would pass and things would return to normal. Yet, looking back, it was around this time that I became aware of the small cracks in our family life.

Dad had managed to get some shifts with a local cab firm and he jumped at the opportunity to earn some much-needed money. Then one day he simply vanished. Vicky and I continually asked Mum where he had gone. She would reply that he was working away. We accepted this explanation at first, but the days went by and there was still no sign. It seemed like an eternity since we'd last seen him.

It was confusing. He was here one day and gone the next. Mum looked so worried and I missed him so much. I didn't know whether he'd come to some harm, was in trouble, or even if he was still alive.

One day Mum got a letter from Dad. I don't know what he wrote, but it made her cry. I'd never seen Mum like this before. She seemed like a broken woman. Resigned. Now that I'm an adult myself I realise that back then they were simply vulnerable human beings with feelings.

I was old enough to be aware there was something wrong, but Mum was careful about what she said in front of Vicky and me. No matter how much I tried to eavesdrop, I couldn't find out what was going on.

Then another letter arrived, and when Mum had finished reading it, she handed it to me. The note was written on a strange-coloured lined paper, not like the small writing pad Mum had in the house. On the back of it was my name.

'Dear Sharon,' it read. 'I hope you are being a good girl and that you are helping your mum and Vicky. I miss you and will see you very soon.'

'Where is he, Mum?' I asked, tears welling up.

She just looked at me with sad eyes and said: 'Everything is okay. Your dad will be home soon.'

After a few weeks I came to accept the fact that he wasn't at home any more, and it became the norm. Vicky was too young to understand what was going on, and she had no real concept of time. She probably thought he'd popped out to the shops for cigarettes. I suppose as children you accept situations as long as they do not impact on your own life too much.

Then one day he suddenly turned up again. He simply

walked in unannounced through the front door as if nothing had happened. I ran towards him and gave him a huge hug and a kiss. Soon I just stopped asking where he had been during that time. What was the point? He was home again.

*

Christine Brown, our babysitter, was the best in the village. Although she was just 14 years old, she was in great demand. Other kids' parents would try to hire her at weekends, but Mum always seemed to get priority. Vicky must have been just months old, and I was just four when Christine started babysitting us. She was a young, vibrant, self-assured teenager who I was immediately in awe of. She seemed so grown-up and confident for her age; she could have easily passed for 16 or 17.

Mum had always found it difficult to find a babysitter that she liked, and she had tried so many different girls before Christine, but whether it was because we played up, or they just simply weren't suitable, none of them seemed to last for any length of time.

It was the same routine every time Mum and Dad wanted to go out. Vicky would cry and I would moan, and often there were tears and tantrums as they kissed us goodbye. But as soon as I knew that it was Christine who would be babysitting us, I became calm. For us, she was the best babysitter in the world, and, if we couldn't be with Mum and Dad, then Christine was a good second best.

Christine lived in the same street, so she was always on hand and was usually available at short notice. She was never short of ideas to keep us occupied, and often she would take us on adventure walks. We especially loved it if she took us to see the horse at the farm down the road from the house. It was a fair old trek, usually through thick mud, to get there, but so rewarding when we arrived and we were able to feed the horse carrots which we'd 'borrowed' from the kitchen.

She also taught us a lot about art, and spent ages sitting with us and drawing horses and dogs. She was very talented and would sketch them out so that I could colour in the images, and Vicky could do her 'baby scribbles' on the page. When she arrived at the house to look after us she was never empty-handed. She always brought a goody bag crammed full of crisps and chocolates. She would have the patience to play any games with us that we wanted, and often they continued for hours on end. She let us stay up way past our bedtime, and sometimes, exhausted and happy, Vicky and I would fall asleep on the couch cuddling into her.

It was as if Christine was always there back then. Mum loved her and they had a great rapport together. She increasingly looked upon her as part of the family.

Christine must have been a godsend for Mum. She finally had a babysitter she and Dad trusted and that we were happy with. It wasn't long before Mum and Dad were so used to having Christine around that they began to organise the odd weekend away together. It was arranged that it would be better if Christine moved in for the weekend – to look after us in our own home and our initial disappointment at not going away with our parents was tempered by the prospect of a whole weekend with Christine – and the fact that Mum and Dad would bring us back a souvenir from their short holiday.

On one such weekend I ran downstairs from my bedroom to find Christine in the kitchen making toast. She suddenly asked me if I liked her cooking. 'Of course,' I replied. She then asked, 'Do you think I am a better cook than your mum?' It was probably asked in innocence, but looking back now, it has more significance: it was as if she was trying to slip into the role of surrogate mother. But she could never, ever replace our mum.

Christine started popping in after she'd finished school most days, and regularly took Vicky and me for long walks to let Mum get on with the housework. I loved going out with her. She was like the big sister I never had.

There were also times when we went out as a family, and Christine came along too. She met all my family, my aunts and uncles. Everyone thought she was just perfect.

After Dad's short spell working the taxis, my uncle Ian – Mum's brother – managed to arrange it for him to get a job at the local bakery as a delivery driver. This wasn't the first time my uncle had stepped in to help the family. He was our Good Samaritan, lending money when things were tight.

It's funny how silly incidents stick in your mind. It is so trivial, but one such occasion still hurts me today. It was the morning of my sixth birthday, and I rushed downstairs before anyone else was up. I opened the fridge to get a drink. Imagine my delight when I saw it was laden full of cakes from Dad's bakery. There was everything from chocolate éclairs and meringues to trifles and fairy cakes. I immediately, and perhaps not unnaturally, thought they were for a surprise birthday party for me, so I didn't mention anything to Mum, went off cheerily to school that morning and promptly invited all my friends to my house for a party later that day.

I was so excited I couldn't wait to get home to put on my party dress. When I came downstairs dressed in my best frock, my mum said I wasn't having a party and that when my friends turned up it was down to me to explain to them. This was out of character for Mum, and it was unusual for her to speak so sharply to me. I was hurt, but her tone was such that I didn't dare argue.

It was never explained to me why our fridge was full of cakes and goodies, but it was the most embarrassing moment of my childhood, and the one day I felt let down by both my parents.

It was around this time that Vicky set fire to our house. Vicky was nearly three when she found my dad's broken cigarette lighter and started to play with it. Although he had discarded it because it wouldn't work, it sparked into life suddenly, setting fire to some of my schoolbooks which were on Vicky's bed.

I remember sitting in the living room when I noticed the smoke creeping down the stairs. Then Mum started screaming that the house was on fire. She and I headed for the front door, but we couldn't see Vicky. Mum frantically began searching the house, eventually finding her a few minutes later at the back of the big cupboard in the kitchen. She'd realised she was in big trouble and had immediately hidden.

Afterwards the house was in a terrible state. All we saved from our room was a wardrobe. Our bunk beds were ashes and all our toys were melted lumps of plastic. We had to continue living there until it was repaired, and I still remember to this day the terrible stench of burning wood.

The fire ripped apart my home, the house I loved so much. I was devastated. Vicky and I both had terrible nightmares about the fire, and I know that day left us emotionally scarred. From that day on I have been terrified of fire.

*

As if things couldn't get much worse, Dad was laid off work again. The bakery he worked for had gone bust: one day he had a well-paid job; the next he didn't.

Mum, ever the worrier, began to fret about the practical things – paying bills and having enough money to buy food. Dad insisted it was a temporary setback and declared: 'The Hamiltons will be back to normal soon enough.'

Our relatives helped us as much as possible and gave us cash handouts whenever they could afford to. I remember having to go and ask Gran for a loan of some money – perhaps Mum and Dad couldn't face the shame of going cap in hand. But I knew I had to do it; we desperately needed the money.

Dad was true to his word, and within a few weeks managed to secure a job back on the taxis. He used to do wedding hire, and I remember him standing on a Saturday morning with the ironing board out, pressing the crisp white linen sheets that would cover the back seat of the car. He was obsessive about making sure his car was clean, and he would also proudly attach beautiful white ribbons to the front of his car before setting off to pick up the wedding party. He worked long shifts so he wasn't there much, but once again money was coming into the house. I thought things were starting to look up.

Chapter Three

IT WAS A Sunday at the height of summer and a much-anticipated day in the social calendar in Redding; a charity fund-raising event at the local working-men's club. The villagers were trying to raise money for a young local lad who needed an electric wheelchair. In situations like this Redding pulls together as one, and everybody was keen to do their bit to help. It seemed that the entire village had bought tickets, and Mum and Dad were getting ready to walk along to the club.

Suddenly the phone rang. It was Christine. She had been babysitting Vicky and me for about two years and it had become a regular arrangement, particularly at weekends, but she told Mum she couldn't babysit us that day because she'd managed to get a ticket for the event, and wanted to go along too.

'Ask one of her sisters,' Dad shouted to Mum after she'd relayed the message to him. Christine's older sister Linda agreed to come round.

Linda arrived within minutes, and almost as soon as she had walked through the door, Mum and Dad kissed us goodbye, and headed off to the charity event. We wouldn't see them for hours.

I could tell straight away that Linda didn't appear too happy about being left to babysit us, and she sat sulking in the living room while Vicky and I played with our toys in our bedroom.

It was early evening but still light outside when Vicky and I heard a commotion outside our house. We were in our room playing with our dolls when we were aware of shouting and screaming from the street below. I ran to the window, but couldn't see a thing. Then, from downstairs I heard our front door burst open with a loud crash.

I ran out of our bedroom to the top of the stairs. Vicky was right behind me, holding on to me for dear life. We still couldn't see what was happening, so we crept down the stairs. At the bottom, I stood motionless, as I tried to take in the chaotic scene. The hall was full of people; mostly relatives. In the middle of them all I could see Mum and Christine shouting at each other at the tops of their voices. They both looked a mess. Christine's normally long, glossy hair looked like rats' tails, as if she'd been caught in a downpour; Mum's mascara was running down her face. She'd been crying. Her cheeks were red and angry.

At first, nobody noticed us standing there, and I took Vicky's hand and tried to squeeze through people's legs to get to the living room where Mum and Christine were continuing their row. I shouted for Mum at the top of my voice, and it suddenly went silent as people turned to look at Vicky and me.

Mum ran over to us and gave us a hug, telling us to go back to our room. Someone tried to prise me from Mum's arms. 'I want to stay here with you,' I remember pleading.

It was the first time I had ever seen Mum and Christine row. I'd never even heard them exchange a cross word before that day but it was not going to be the last. Later that night Vicky and I were both suddenly wakened again by the sound of people shouting outside our room – we now had twin beds instead of bunk beds but, because we were so scared, Vicky slept in my bed that night. Then, our bedroom door was pushed open. 'Get away from my children. Get away from my children.' It was Mum and she sounded distressed. Then Mum and Christine were in our room. I sat bolt upright in bed and Vicky was cuddling into me and trembling.

Christine walked up to the bed and leaned over us. I could smell alcohol and cigarettes from the pub. 'Tell your mum you love me,' she said. I was bewildered and scared; I didn't know what to say. I looked at her, and then Mum. Then Mum just screamed.

Suddenly Dad was in the room and shouted at both Mum and Christine to get down the stairs.

Over the following days, slowly, through snatches of conversation between Mum and some of our relatives, I became aware of my father and Christine's affair. At the charity event, Christine had met Mum in the toilets and blurted out that she and Dad – or Mike as she called him – were having a relationship.

Only years later was I able to look back and realise that the signs of their secret relationship were more than obvious. There was the time when Mum called Christine to ask her to babysit until my dad got home from work as she had to go out for an appointment. Christine duly obliged and waited with us in the house until Dad returned. When I came downstairs from my room, my dad was sitting in his big armchair in front of the TV with Christine sat at his feet. I noticed that Dad was gently stroking her hair; twisting her locks in his fingers as if it was the most natural thing in the world.

Looking back, Mum didn't stand a chance against this friendly, outgoing, confident girl who was half my father's age. He must have been flattered by her attention, and she, still an impressionable schoolgirl of 16, must have been in awe of him; an older worldly-wise man with a good job and money.

I was devastated by my father's affair. Vicky was simply

too young to fully understand. She witnessed the rows and the shouting, but didn't realise the situation or that our parents' marriage was ending.

I was six years old when Dad's relationship with Christine became public, and although I didn't understand fully what was going on, I was concerned about my mum. I saw how unhappy she was and wanted to do what I could to comfort her. She always seemed to be in tears, and I think I grew up a lot myself in the early weeks of my parents' separation. I knew my dad had upset my mum, but I still loved him dearly, and hoped that things would be good again. And that the rows and tears would finally stop.

*

As if this period in my life wasn't traumatic and upsetting enough, I had to contend with another confusing situation, one that, because of my tender years, I didn't fully understand.

A friend of the family – a boy of around 11 or 12 – was beginning to pay me some attention. I didn't really comprehend what he was doing. He was always around my house, and Vicky and I would often be at his home. It started with a game of Postman's Knock. There would be a group of us, and he would encourage us to go into various rooms for kissing and cuddling.

One time I was among a group of about seven children at his mother's house. He said he wanted to play a game of doctors and nurses. I had a toy doctor's case with a syringe and a stethoscope at home, and I often played the same game with Vicky. So when he suggested playing, I agreed.

He was very cunning. He tricked me into playing a different 'version' of the game by telling me I had to take all my clothes off. He took his top and trousers off too and told me to lie on top of him and rub myself against him. I didn't realise what he was doing, but I did feel uncomfortable. I knew it was wrong, but I didn't know why. I didn't like the way he was making me feel. Then he firmly took hold of my wrist and pushed my hand towards his private parts. I had never seen a penis before, and certainly not an erect one.

Afterwards, he told me that we had to keep our game a secret and tell nobody – especially my mum and dad – because I would get into trouble. I believed him and said nothing. It had become my secret too, and because I hadn't told anyone it began happening more and more. He would invite a group of other children round to his house, usually to listen to music. I was always invited. I thought I'd be all right going to his house in a group, but he was always smarter than me, and managed to engineer a situation where we would be alone together. But, after everyone left and I said I would have to go too, he would take my hand and gently pull me back into his room, with an excuse that he wanted to talk to me about something, or that he had something to show me.

His room is still vivid in my mind; the walls and furniture covered with Elvis Presley memorabilia; posters, albums, books and magazines. Then it would happen all over again.

It got to the stage where I dreaded seeing him, but it was very difficult to avoid him in our tiny village. He was little more than a child himself, and he was always hanging around our street – and our home.

It was impossible for me to hide from his wandering hands. I would make excuses to leave the room if he was in it, but he would always follow. He just wouldn't take no for an answer. I wanted to scream at him to get lost, but I was ultimately too scared; and I would physically freeze when he touched me. He never penetrated me; he was far too clever for that.

I thought I could cope with the situation. I believed that eventually he would lose interest. But he didn't, even when he managed to get a girlfriend. It was still happening. I felt what he was doing was wrong, but I still couldn't pluck up the courage to tell Mum or Dad. They had their own problems, and were barely speaking.

I was trying to cope with their constant rowing and living in an unhappy home, and now I was being sexually abused. I was a very confused little girl, with nobody to turn to for help. I was desperately unhappy.

Then, out of the blue, Mum told me one day that the boy and his mother were moving away. She must have wondered why a huge broad grin spread across my face after she said this. Inside my heart was jumping for joy. No more abuse; no more mind games.

By the time he left the abuse had been going on for years. It wasn't constant, but whenever he could he engineered a situation where we would be together, and he always managed to get me on my own. Strangely, in the year before he emigrated, he didn't try anything, which I was very relieved about.

I still kept the secret of what he did to me, even when he left Redding in the mid-eighties. I buried that awful experience deep into the recesses of my mind.

*

Dad lived between two women after his affair was uncovered; my mum and Christine, and my family life became confusing and disjointed.

Mum would later tell me that despite his affair, he insisted he still loved her. But he said he couldn't give up Christine. I lost count of the number of times Dad left the house after Mum and he had a blazing row.

After one particularly distressing argument Mum

decided to leave the family home. She must have managed to contact the social work department, because I can remember the three of us being bundled into a car while a woman, who I later found out was a social worker, drove around Falkirk trying to find us a bed for the night. We were all crying as we sat huddled in the back of the car.

We stopped at a house in Camelon on the outskirts of the town. Mum whispered to me that it was a refuge, and explained what that meant. But, after the social worker spoke to someone at the door, she returned to tell us that there were no spare beds.

Then we arrived at a house back in town. We were invited in, but Mum said she felt uneasy about the place and said she wanted to try elsewhere.

We got back into the car and the social worker asked if we had any relatives who would help us for the night, but Mum said it was only my dad's family who lived locally and the only ones she felt able to ask were my dad's brother John and his wife Sandra. They were aware of Mum and Dad's marital problems, but were good people, and unlikely to take sides.

We drove back to Redding, and pulled up outside Uncle John's. The social worker was about to leave us in the car to go and explain the situation to John and Sandra when Mum suddenly proclaimed: 'We're going back home.'

She had a look of determination on her face; it was as if she had realised that it was *her* home too and no matter how difficult it was becoming for her to live with my dad she still had every right to be there. The social worker had a long chat with Mum before we got out of the car.

We walked along the road and into Woodburn Avenue. Mum went ahead and walked around the house, looking for signs of life. All the lights were off. She quietly unlocked the front door and crept into the hallway, leaving us on the steps.

Dad wasn't home. We could go in. I lay in my bed that night crying. I cannot remember ever feeling so scared and unhappy.

*

For months Dad lived what can only be described as a fractured lifestyle; spending most of the time away from the family home, only returning occasionally. I'm not sure where he slept while he was away, but Vicky and I almost got used to this unusual domestic situation. It was probably down to the age difference between us, but Vicky still wanted to see Dad, and never asked any difficult questions of him; I wanted nothing to do with him.

I learned later from Mum that Christine and Dad's affair had been continuing on and off for about five years. During this time he had boomeranged between the two women, sometimes spending weeks on end at our house, at other times living with Christine. He would turn up at our house and Mum would let him in. She told me she just couldn't give him up. I think she always hoped that one day he would stay for good. Then he would row with Mum and go back to Christine.

One day when Vicky was about five, she turned up at our house with a dog. She said Christine had given him to her as a present. Mum was fuming. I think she saw it as a form of blackmail by Christine; an attempt to win Vicky over and keep contact with her. But Vicky was so happy with Shane the dog that Mum relented and told Vicky she could keep him. Vicky and Shane were inseparable, and she and I would sneak him upstairs into our bedroom at night with our other dog Patch – until we were caught by Mum. It was just the excuse she needed, and she decreed that though Vicky could keep Shane, he wasn't allowed in the house.

Shane followed Vicky everywhere. He even met her outside the school gates, and together they walked across the road and into *that* house opposite where Dad and Christine lived. I walked on. Vicky and Shane dropped in to Dad's house all the time. She was a confused little girl, and her world was in turmoil. She just wanted to be loved by everyone, I suppose.

Then the roof caved in on Vicky's little world – again.

One night Vicky and I were playing in our garden when a girl shouted to us something about Shane and a car. Vicky immediately bolted from the garden and ran along the road with the girl as I followed behind. We ran to the railway bridge on Redding Road about four hundred yards from our house. Vicky arrived at the scene before me, and I found her on her knees on the road. Shane was lying there looking up at her as she cradled his head and kissed his face. There was a small crowd around them and one of the local boys said Shane had run into the road right into the path of a car. My heart broke for Vicky. She had been through so much in the last few months. She had been fighting for both Mum and Dad's affections, looking desperately for an answer to why her little world had been turned upside down.

It sounds silly now, but I think Vicky channelled what real love she had to Shane, her pet dog. Now he lay close to dying on her lap as she kissed him goodbye, and I felt nothing but pure love for my little sister.

*

Then, astonishingly, Mum and Dad announced they were going into business together. Dad had bought a fast food van in which he said he would sell fish and chips. Mum was to be his partner.

This happened during a spell when Dad was staying

with us and not Christine, and Vicky and I saw this as a glimmer of hope, a sign that perhaps Dad had finally made his decision and was going to move back home permanently.

For a while things went well and Mum spent her days preparing food which Dad sold on his rounds in the evening. The venture seemed to be a success and Mum appeared happier than I had seen her for a while.

But one night when Dad was out on his rounds with the van Mum asked me to go on my bike, find Dad and give him a note. She was able to work out he would be in Westquarter by this time and gave me an idea what street he was likely to be in.

When I arrived in the village, it didn't take me long to locate the van. I peddled up to the side door, squeezed past a couple of customers and entered the van. Christine was behind the counter wrapping chips. I was shocked but I said nothing, passed Dad the note from Mum and left straight away.

When I got home, Mum immediately asked the question I was dreading: 'Was Christine in the van?' She must have known all along, but was looking for confirmation. I couldn't bring myself to tell her, but the look on my face must have said it all.

It didn't take Mum long to confront Dad when he got home, and Vicky and I were woken by the sound of more shouting from downstairs. Dad finally moved out, this time for good.

*

'Why are we moving house, Mum?' I asked.

'Because our house is sinking and it is being pulled down,' she replied.

I didn't want to leave our family home. It was the house of my childhood, and there had been many good times there. Many times I had longed for our family to be back the way it was, not broken and fragmented as it was now, and the house represented that earlier family for me.

There was subsidence in our street, and some of the houses were due to be knocked down because they were deemed to be unsafe. The local council had been trying for months to find us alternative accommodation, but nothing suitable had come up. Then a small two-bedroom flat came up for rent and Mum said she would take it. The council told her it was only temporary until something bigger became available.

It just didn't feel like home when we moved in. Only the three of us – Mum, Vicky and me. None of us really wanted to admit it, but we missed Dad so much. Vicky and I knew Mum had cried a lot every time Dad left over the preceding months, so maybe she thought: 'A new home. A new start.' I was 12, and Vicky eight. Mum had at last accepted that Dad had opted for a new life with Christine. It was time for her to move on.

The flat was cosy with a traditional coal fire that the three of us huddled round on cold winter nights; sometimes making toast with bread balanced on long forks. The bedrooms were big and comfortable. Mum didn't have much money, and was still using the double bed she and Dad had shared as a married couple. Vicky and I shared a room.

Mum found it hard to adjust to her new life. I suppose it wasn't really so new; just like the old life, but without Dad. The only people she really had to talk to were Vicky and me, and her sisters and brother. She'd lost trust in many of her old friends, some of whom had taken Dad's side after the split.

It was confusing for Vicky and me too. When we walked together to Christine's flat where Dad was now living I always felt incredibly sad; sad for myself. I would be visiting my father and the woman who I came to love when she was my babysitter. Here I was in *their* home. The house they shared together and to which Vicky and I didn't really belong.

I may have been a child, but I knew exactly what had happened, and I, of course, sided with my mother, who I felt had been betrayed.

I knew how Mum felt, because I felt it too. I saw

something die in her when Dad left for good. I still loved my Dad despite everything, and I was fighting my feelings for Christine. She was only ten years older than me, and here she was making a home with my father.

Vicky was still young and oblivious to a lot that had gone on. I could tell she loved her dad, and still had strong feelings for Christine too. But I knew that one day Vicky would start asking awkward questions. And then it would be time for her to make her own mind up.

*

As often happens when families break up, inevitably one of the main points of contention is money. Mum never seemed to have much, although she never complained, and she still managed to provide Vicky and me with what we wanted. Whenever we needed some extra money and Mum couldn't give it to us, we set off on the 15-minute walk to Dad and Christine's flat in Westquarter.

I found it hard to ask my dad for anything, even just 20p. But going to Dad's house to ask for extra money was a journey we made many times in the first two years after the split. Mum would never ask us to, but we always seemed to realise when things were tight, and set off in the hope that we would catch him in a good frame of mind. If it was daylight, we walked down the 'fairy steps', but when it was dark we stuck to the main road, which was longer but not so scary at night-time. When we arrived he never offered to spend time with us; never asked us if we wanted to visit the park. I often thought he just handed us some money to make us disappear off back home and leave him in peace with his new girlfriend. Our days of fun with our dad, when he would take us out on our bicycles, or just for a walk, were gone. They ended the day he walked out the door for good. It broke my heart.

Once Mum seemed to have it all; married to a man she adored, two daughters, a nice house and many friends. Now she was in a small two-bedroom flat living on the doorstep of where her marriage fell apart. Mum always told us that Dad never gave her any money to run her house or buy things for us, but I can't know if that was the case for sure. She always seemed to be the one who was scrimping and saving to buy our school shoes. She always seemed to be the one who suffered most.

We watched Mum stretch the little money she had to make ends meet. Sometimes she would literally count every penny in her purse to work out what she could afford.

One day, just a few weeks after we had moved into the flat, two men turned up at the front door. They had arrived to take our colour television away. Vicky and I got upset, but soon resigned ourselves to watching the black-

and-white one instead and simply using our imagination to work out what the colours would be.

Christmas 1983 – the first in the new flat – was miserable. Mum had little or no money left after paying all the bills, so she was unable to buy Vicky and me many presents. I think our financial situation really hit home then, because at all previous Christmas times when Dad was still in the house, we had got piles of gifts, and we had been really spoiled.

Mum was so desperate to give us a good Christmas she went begging to social services who helped her as much as they could by giving her second-hand clothes and games.

Two weeks after Christmas Day Dad turned up with a present for Vicky and me. It was the first time he had set foot in our flat since he had moved in with Christine. He gave us our gifts and a kiss and a cuddle and asked Vicky and me to go outside to play while he and Mum had a chat. Naively I thought this was a sign they were going to get back together, so no sooner had his request left his lips than we had our hats and coats on and we were off outside. Vicky and I played under the street lights on our roller skates. All the time I wondered what being said inside the house. I think I knew it was our last hope.

I don't remember how long we played for, but it was after our bedtime and dark when Mum called us back in. When we got home, he was gone.

*

A few weeks later Vicky and I caught Mum crying in the kitchen. 'What's wrong, Mum?' I asked.

The tears were rolling down her face. 'I've got something to tell you both,' she said. 'I'm pregnant.'

'You should be happy,' I said.

My first reaction was perhaps in hindsight a strange one, but other people seemed happy when they were pregnant and I was truly delighted about what she had just told me.

I suppose it was a bit of a shock and I hadn't really thought about how it could have happened. As far as I knew, Mum hadn't been seeing anyone else, so she must have been with Dad – probably while we were out playing on our roller skates that day.

'You don't understand, Sharon. You're too young,' she sobbed. 'I can't bring this child up, Sharon. He or she will grow up without a father.'

'Maybe this will bring you and Dad back together again,' I said.

'That will never ever happen,' she added. 'Your dad and I are getting divorced. He has made his choice.'

It was the first time the word divorce was used, and it should have come as a shock as it would be the final chapter in my mum and dad's marriage, but I was just happy to hear the news that Mum was expecting. I looked

Mum in the eye and said: 'Vicky and I will help you. I'm thirteen. I'm old enough to help.'

The next few weeks were happy ones. All Vicky and I could talk about was Mum's baby. Vicky just kept saying she was going to be a big sister; not a little one any more. We were going to have another person joining our family, and we couldn't wait.

Mum was very guarded about what Dad's reaction had been when she told him the news, and he even seemed to be avoiding Vicky and me. I arrived home from school one day to find Mum in the kitchen crying again. I asked her what was wrong.

'I went to the hospital today for my scan and the nurse asked me a strange question. She asked me how many babies I would like. I joked with her and told her I wasn't sure if I even wanted one, and she told me: "Mrs Hamilton, you are having twins."

'I thought she was having a laugh, but she showed me two heart beats on the computer screen.'

I was shocked to hear this news, but remember wondering where they would sleep. We only had two bedrooms. And even at that age I knew two more people in the family would stretch the little money we had even further.

Then I pulled myself together. 'Mum. We will get by, like we always do,' I said.

'But that's not all, Sharon,' she said. 'Christine is

pregnant too, and she's due to have her baby at the same time as me.'

I now know Mum considered ending the pregnancy, but I think this was just an impulse reaction to the shock of hearing the news about the twins and Christine. Within a few days she was back to being her practical self, and planning for the births with our help.

We spent weeks saving money and getting things ready for the new arrivals: two cots; loads of blankets; Mum even managed to get her hands on a second-hand twin pram. She took up knitting again and produced a wardrobe full of cardigans and tops for the babies.

During the entire nine months I saw neither hide nor hair of my dad. I asked Mum a couple of times if he had been in touch, but she just changed the subject as soon as I raised it. It was as if nothing had changed. He still had his new life with Christine, and we were left to struggle on, financially and emotionally.

It was great to see Mum being positive. It was as if the pregnancy had given her a new purpose in life, and she knew Vicky and I would do whatever we could to help. She even allowed each of us to choose a name for the babies – although we didn't even know what gender they were yet.

Mum was booked in for a Caesarian section at Falkirk Royal Infirmary on 17 September 1984, and I set off for school that day with feelings of excitement and trepidation. I didn't have to wait long into my school day until one of the teachers came to my classroom and told me that the twins had been born. The school arranged for me to leave class and go to the hospital to visit Mum.

When I got to the maternity ward Mum was still groggy from the anaesthetic, so the nurse said she would take me to the side room where my brother and sister were. Did she just say brother? I have a little brother? I just couldn't stop smiling. I couldn't wait to tell Mum that finally she had a son. I knew she wanted one and that she would be so happy.

I peered into the two cots that were side by side in the room and looked at my beautiful new brother and sister.

When I was eventually allowed into the ward to see Mum she was still very drowsy. I kissed her and she tried to smile, but the tears were rolling down her cheeks. I decided that the boy was to be called Lee, and Vicky decided on Lindsay for the girl. Our new family had just grown by two overnight.

Mum was released from hospital a few days later, so Vicky and I raced home from our respective schools – I was at the local Graeme High School now – desperate to see the twins. We both rushed in the door at the same time, and came to a complete halt at the scene before us in the living room. Dad was in the flat.

Not only was he in our house, but he was laughing and

joking and fussing over the two tiny bundles which he had spread across his arms. I remember wishing I had a camera to hand.

There was a huge grin on his face. 'Meet your brother and sister,' he said to us. I looked at Mum and she was grinning too – and glowing with pride. Although it was strange to see him, by then I knew him too well to think for one second that he planned to come back properly into our lives.

Mum was exhausted and unable to do any lifting or physical tasks while she was recovering from her operation. Over the next couple of days I watched Dad come back and forth to the house, doing errands for Mum, even sorting the twins' milk and nappies. He went to the local registry office to register the births – Lee Michael (after himself) and Lindsay Helen (after Mum's sister).

It was strange for Vicky and me having Dad around the house again. Christine was never mentioned, at least not in front of us.

Then on 27 September – ten days after the twins were born – Christine gave birth to a daughter called Nicole. Dad didn't darken our doorstep again.

*

The following week the twin buggy was delivered to the flat. After it arrived I asked Mum if I could take Lee and

Lindsay out in it for a walk. I didn't tell Mum where I was going, because she wouldn't have let me go, but I was heading for Dad's house. I had decided he was going to see his children again even if I had to take them to him.

The twins looked a bit squashed in their new buggy, but cosy as I pushed them down the fairy steps towards Dad's house. Then a pebble got caught in one of the wheels and the buggy tipped spilling the twins face first on to the gravel. I pulled the buggy upright and saw the twins' grazed and bruised heads. There was blood trickling down their cheeks and they were both crying. I screamed for help, but there was nobody nearby.

I was only around 80 yards from Dad's house, so I unfastened the twins from the buggy, tucked one under each arm and ran towards the house. When I got there the front door was ajar. I shouted up the stairs towards an open door at the top. Christine appeared and asked what all the fuss was about. Before I could explain, she saw I had the twins with me and refused to let me into the house.

I turned away, collected the buggy, and headed for home.

When I got home and told Mum what had happened she went berserk at me, mainly for going to Dad's behind her back. I told her that I had wanted him to see his children. We had a huge fallout; one of the worst we ever had.

Chapter Four

I HAVE, SINCE I was young enough to remember, always been fiercely protective of Vicky.

When she started at my school – Westquarter Primary – I was nine and in Primary Four. The large white building must have appeared daunting to any five-year-old turning up on their first day. Vicky was scared, but also excited about joining me at the 'big school.' She was one of the lucky ones having her big sister there to look after her and show her the ropes.

The school had separate playgrounds; her section filled with Primaries One, Two and Three pupils, and mine at the 'senior' end of the school – eight-year-olds and upwards. I suppose the reason for that was to keep the smaller children away from the rough-and-tumble games of the older pupils to stop them being knocked over and hurt.

Every day during morning and lunchtime breaks I would walk round to Vicky's playground to see her and make sure she was okay. I needn't have fretted. It was marvellous to witness Vicky's social skills, even for a child so young. With her outgoing personality, it didn't take Vicky long to make new friends. She had a certain cheeky charm which made her so lovable. With her huge blue eyes, chubby cheeks and tousled brown hair, she looked the epitome of cute; as if butter wouldn't melt in her mouth.

She was also a bit of a star pupil. While I was content to sit and colour in a book or play with a doll, Vicky would choose to sit and read quietly. I never had a great love for books, but Vicky just devoured them. As a result, she always did really well at school, and became one of the teacher's pets. Her teacher would boast about Vicky's achievements in school to Mum whenever she saw her. She thought Vicky had great potential and said she was a joy to teach.

As her big sister I should have been proud of her, but I have to admit I felt a little jealous. She began to get all the attention from both Mum and Dad, and I found it annoying. I felt left out as it seemed they both cuddled and praised Vicky at every opportunity.

At that time, Dad and I had had a real father-daughter bond, and now I seemed to be gradually losing it. He preferred to play with Vicky rather than me now, and looking back, I suppose I can't really blame him. I was a timid child given to moaning, or whingeing, and I didn't like to play rough and tumble in case I got hurt. I suppose

I was a girlie girl while Vicky was more of a tomboy. I'd rather watch than join in, while Vicky was the life and soul; the girl with an infectious, hearty laugh. When you heard it, you just had to join in.

*

After Mum and Dad's break-up I felt it was my duty to look after Vicky, and there is no doubt that our sisterly bond was truly cemented during those difficult years. While our parents were verbally knocking lumps out of each other, Vicky and I would retreat to our bedroom and play together.

I suppose it was inevitable that as Vicky progressed through school she would make new friends – something she did with consummate ease. Gradually her big sister didn't seem quite so important. We still got on well, but she would have other girls to call on, and often, especially during the summer months, she would be outside with her schoolchums playing in the street or the local park.

If truth be told, I had new interests too – and new friends – and before long Vicky and I had the kind of relationship that most siblings with a three- or four-year age difference have: one of tolerance and mild embarrassment.

I grew into a teenager with teenage attitudes and friends my own age. Mini adults, I suppose, and the four-year age gulf between us suddenly seemed like more. I sort of stumbled my way through school, not doing brilliantly, but not doing that badly either. I discovered boys while Vicky was just discovering pop music. It got to the point that we sometimes only really communicated with each other at mealtimes. I don't think this was particularly unusual; it was simply that we had separate lives and they were being lived in parallel to each other.

I also had a plan which would tragically impact on both our lives. At the age of 17 I decided to leave home.

*

My mum was the most precious person in the world to me, so telling her I planned to leave the family home was a traumatic and heartbreaking experience.

Mum seemed to be resigned to her role as a single parent and worked day and night in the house to provide for me, Vicky and the twins. I was 17 and bored, fed up with the predictability of home life. I needed a new adventure. It was a big wide world out there, and I wanted to experience it.

I'd been secretly planning to move to Livingston, a town between Redding and Edinburgh. I'd met a boy named Scott who had his own flat in Livingston, and within a few months of us meeting up he'd asked me to move in with him. It was the chance of freedom I'd been longing for.

Mum didn't quite see it that way, and she was furious when I told her my plans. She said she couldn't believe I wanted to walk away from her, Vicky, Lee and Lindsay, especially for a boy she felt I hardly knew. I was devastated and shocked by the strength of her reaction. She was all but pleading with me to stay.

Perhaps she saw my plan to leave as a further erosion of her family. Dad had left, and I'm sure she couldn't face the prospect of someone else leaving her. I felt torn; split between loyalty to my mum and my determination to strike out on my own and escape from my mundane life.

Ironically, my relationship with my dad had improved considerably over the previous couple of years, and although he never visited the family home any more, Vicky and I visited him. I decided to tell Dad about my plans, fully expecting him to be against the idea and to try and stop me from leaving Mum – it would help salve his conscience if I was still around to help Mum with Vicky and the twins.

His reaction still surprises me: 'Do what you want to do, Sharon,' he told me. There were no lectures. Even Christine chipped in saying that Mum couldn't stop me from going, and if I left there was nothing she could do about it as I was 17 and, in Scotland, that meant I was legally an adult. I left Dad's house hoping that Mum would maybe change her mind once I told her that he had given me his blessing. But she just wouldn't budge.

I knew Mum relied on me a great deal. I helped her with the twins, with the housework and shouldered some of the burden of bringing up a young family. Three years earlier I'd promised her before the twins were born that I would support her as much as I could, but now as a 17-year-old I was beginning to resent the burden she was placing on my shoulders. I was just out of school, working full time and I was spending most of my spare time in the house. I needed to break free from my monotonous routine.

I worked for a local supermarket, and my plans to move out were strengthened when they offered me a position in their main store in Livingston. It was the extra push I needed.

The night I finally decided to leave Redding was traumatic – for me and for Mum. Mum was angry, and she didn't try to hide it. I stood in front of her, Vicky and the twins with just a black bin liner filled with my clothes and personal possessions. I kissed Lee and Lindsay tenderly on their cheeks, then I gave Vicky a huge hug. I joked with her that at last she could have the bedroom we had shared all to herself.

This was a huge moment in my life. At the time I thought Mum was being selfish wanting to tie me to the house. I couldn't understand why she couldn't appreciate that all I wanted was my independence and was so dead against my decision. Instead of feeling sorry for her, I got angry too and we had a blazing row. At the height of it Mum delivered an ultimatum: 'If you go to Livingston, you will not be welcome back home.' I told her that was fine by me and walked out without looking back. In finding the independence I craved, I'd lost the one thing that was dear to me – my family.

Scott and I were sublimely happy, but shortly after I moved in, he was made redundant. Times were tough and money was extremely tight, but I was determined I wouldn't crawl back to Mum for help. I was too proud – and stubborn. I had a multitude of jobs that were diverse to say the least: graphic designer, barmaid, pottery-shop worker and glamour model. Scott tried so hard to get another job, filling in one application after another while I tried to run the flat on little or no money, a skill I'd undoubtedly learned from my mum who had to struggle financially all those years after my father left home. This wasn't my idea of fun, but we were a couple and we had a house to keep. My first real house of my own.

After seven months of Mum and I having no contact I swallowed my pride and wrote to her. By then I realised that Mum was simply being protective of the family unit when I decided to leave. I think she was still deeply unhappy with me and our relationship remained strained – and for some time confined to letters – but it was the ice-breaker we both needed.

I also wrote to my best friend Angela and she was able to keep me up to date with what was happening at home as she often visited Mum and occasionally babysat Vicky and the twins. I poured out my heart to her in these letters and told her I missed the family so much, especially little Lee who I had a special bond with. Angela understood and even managed to bring Lee to visit me in Livingston one day.

Occasionally Vicky wrote to me too. She usually wrote about her friends who I didn't really know, but I could tell though her words that she was happy, and seemed to be very popular at school. Our letters became more regular, and Vicky and I found that we had more and more in common. As children I'd always been acutely aware of the four-year age difference between us, but it suddenly didn't seem so wide now. Ironically, we seemed to be getting on better than we did when I was at home fighting with her over our room. I think we were both glad of the independence, and I could sense through her letters that she was becoming a young woman. We ended up exchanging letters almost weekly and building up a great relationship. Mum, for her part, eventually mellowed about me being away. She had made a new friend in Jimmy Graham, a man she had met on a night out. I'd met him before I left and liked him immediately. They seemed to be good for each other.

Dad had also moved on. He and Christine got married at Falkirk Registry Office. It was a very low-key affair, and a difficult day for Mum. Vicky and I were invited, but decided not to go. Seeing Dad marry again, especially to the woman who'd betrayed our mother, was unthinkable.

Eventually I started visiting home again. The atmosphere between Mum and me thawed, and at long last she seemed to accept that I wanted a different life. I tried to visit as much as possible, but I didn't earn a lot of money and I couldn't drive. But on the occasions I did get home, Mum treated me like royalty. She always made her famous home-made broth, and we all sat together for a meal. A happy family again.

Vicky had just turned 14 when Mum took me aside and confessed she was becoming quite concerned about her behaviour. I told her Vicky was just doing what all girls of her age did: discovering boys and experimenting with cigarettes and alcohol. But Mum was scared that Vicky was going off the rails, and it was true, she did seem to have an attitude. Like a typical teenager she had an answer for everything. Mum did everything to keep Vicky on the straight and narrow, but I suppose without a father figure to back her up, and the fact that I wasn't around, she found it a daunting task.

As usual, Mum was right, and it was only a matter of weeks after our conversation that Vicky got into trouble for shoplifting. She was in Falkirk with her friends, and, as was typical of Vicky, she asked them to dare her to steal some aftershave. They did, and she slipped the bottle under her coat before heading for the exit. She got as far as the shop door before one of the assistants confronted her. She and her two friends were marched to see the manager who called the police. They were hardly master criminals, caught at their first attempt at shoplifting, but, instead of being ashamed, Vicky thought the whole episode was a joke.

She and her friends were led through the shop and onto the high street to await the police van. They were taken to Falkirk Police Station where they were locked up in the cells. Vicky *still* thought it was funny. I don't know whether it was bravado, but she was determined not to crack in front of her friends.

The police drove Vicky home later that day, and Mum promptly delivered her a lecture she would never forget. She was grounded for weeks.

Vicky and I led largely separate existences at this point in our lives. I was trying hard to make a go of things in Livingston, and she spent most of her time with her friends. She was a teenager with little to do and often she and her little 'gang' would hang around the streets of Redding, especially during the long summer nights.

Vicky still kept in touch by letter, but it was only years later, after her funeral, that I got a better insight into my sister's all too short teenage years. Her friends Toni, Claire and Leigh went to Graeme High School in Falkirk with Vicky, and they spoke of a happy, carefree girl, full of life and energy. They talked with great affection of visiting her at Mum's house, and of going to Vicky's room – the one we used to share – and of her music posters; Madonna was her favourite. They also spoke of Vicky's love of showjumping, and how she spent weekends at the local stables mucking out the horses. She wasn't paid for this, but the owners in turn allowed her to ride the horses.

Vicky and her friends would sit around for hours chatting about music, make-up and boys. They would often hang around the Redding chip shop, the only real meeting place for teenagers who were too young to go to the local pub.

The girls said Vicky was very popular at school and she started seeing boys, although there was never anyone serious. There was, however, one incident that I only found out about from Mum a couple of years later; Vicky had accused a boy of rape. No one quite knows the full story, and of course, now we never will, but it happened one night when Vicky and a friend went to a club in Falkirk. Vicky had just turned 15 and her friend was 17, although they both looked a lot older.

Both girls had had a fair amount to drink, and they had met a couple of boys they knew from the Falkirk area. Vicky accepted a lift home, but something happened and she was pushed out of the moving car. She was cut on the face and was covered head to toe in bruises.

Later she claimed she was raped by one of the boys. Vicky was questioned by the police about the incident, but a couple of days later she said she wanted to drop the charge against the boy.

At around the same time Vicky's schoolwork started to go downhill. She seemed to have no interest in her classes and it seemed she only attended so she could meet up with her friends. She became the classroom joker and, according to her friends, would expend most of her energies in winding up her teachers.

However, she talked many times of wanting to be a vet. She loved animals, especially horses, so much. Maybe if things hadn't turned out the way they did, she might have buckled down to her studies. She may even have fulfilled her dream.

*

Meanwhile, I was still enjoying my new life in Livingston with Scott, and things became easier financially for us when he eventually found a job in a local factory.

In her last few letters Vicky had written about the possibility of making the journey on her own from Redding to Livingston to spend a few days with me. It was a big deal for her, making the trip unaccompanied, and I vowed to use the extra savings Scott and I had managed to put aside to decorate the spare room, and invite my little sister to stay for the weekend.

Chapter Five

IT IS THE weekend that still, strangely, makes me smile. It is also the weekend that will haunt me for the rest of my life.

It was the happiest two days Vicky and I ever spent together as sisters, and for those precious memories I will always be grateful. But as I hugged and kissed her before she boarded the bus home, I did not know it would be the last time I would ever hold my sister. Her last backwards glance will live with me for ever. I was the last friendly face she ever saw.

*

I recognised the handwriting as I picked the envelope up from the hall carpet. It was a letter from Vicky.

I'd written to her the previous week to finalise plans for her first-ever trip to Livingston to stay with me for the weekend. I'd finished decorating my spare room and it was ready for her to come and stay. I suggested she might bring a friend from school if she wanted to. Vicky was 15.

She'd badgered Mum for weeks to allow her to come and stay with me. I, in turn, had reassured Mum Vicky would be fine and that I would look after her.

I tore open the letter and read Vicky's words. She was planning to come over the following Friday – 8 February – with Leigh, one of her best friends from school. Mum was spending the weekend at her sister's house in Bo'ness, six miles from Falkirk, with the twins to celebrate her fortieth birthday.

I couldn't wait for the weekend to arrive. I was so looking forward to introducing Vicky to all my friends. I just knew they would love her; she was so sociable and fun-loving. She was always great in company and people warmed to her within a few minutes of being with her. Most of all I was looking forward to spending some quality time with my little sister. Normally, I'd only get the chance to catch up with her on the rare occasions I made it to Mum's house, so to have her all to myself in my own flat was going to be fantastic.

I knew how much she'd had to work on Mum to allow her to visit, so I was determined nothing would go wrong, and we would prove to Mum that there was nothing to stop Vicky visiting again. She would be perfectly safe.

For the Friday night I planned that we would stay in and chat, just the three of us over a couple of bottles of wine. Scott had made plans to leave us to ourselves and go out for the night with his friends; he wouldn't have wanted to sit around and listen to us girls gossiping anyway, so I doubt he felt it was a sacrifice! Although Vicky was 15, I knew she and her friends were drinking, and I reckoned there was no point in playing the big sister who preached morals. As long as she drank in moderation I didn't see any harm in it. Besides, I would be looking after the two of them, and there was no way I was going to let either of them get drunk.

On the Saturday I would take the girls to the local Livingston Centre where we could do a bit of shopping, and maybe I could treat Vicky to something nice. It would also give me the chance to buy Mum's birthday present – some earrings I'd promised her. That night we would go to my local pub, the Waverley, where I met my friends most weekends. There was always a disco on a Saturday night, and I knew how much Vicky enjoyed dancing. Although Vicky and Leigh were both under age, they looked much older and I knew there would be no problem getting them into the pub. I couldn't wait to go dancing with Vicky, and I couldn't help smiling to myself as I thought back to the nights we used to creep downstairs during one of Mum and Dad's famous parties and dance in the living room for the amusement of their guests.

On the Sunday I planned to cook them a big breakfast – and probably nurse a hangover.

Work seemed to drag that week. I had changed jobs from the supermarket and was an assistant in a camera shop in Edinburgh. The pay was terrible, and what made it worse was the journey twice a day to and from the shop. It was soul-destroying because of the Edinburgh rush-hour traffic. I managed to beg my boss to allow me to get away early the day Vicky was coming, and I set off for home hoping my bus would beat the 5 p.m. rush. I didn't want Vicky and Leigh turning up on my doorstep unable to get into the flat as I knew how paranoid Vicky was about making sure her journey plan worked out.

I knew they were coming by bus, but they hadn't told me what route they planned to take. They could either catch a bus from Falkirk to Bathgate and then change for Livingston, or they could go the alternative routes via Edinburgh or Linlithgow. Whichever route they were taking, Vicky's letter said she had expected to be at my flat around 7.30 p.m.

I got home at 5.30 p.m, in plenty of time before Vicky and Leigh were due to arrive. I even had time to soak in the bath, and make sure the girls' room was tidy and warm.

I put on some music and waited for the girls to arrive, occasionally checking the street outside through the kitchen window to see if I could spot them walking down the road. Seven thirty came and went, but I wasn't too anxious as the bus services to Livingston could be notoriously late, and it was a bit icy outside, so buses were probably delayed by the weather. I checked through the window again at ten to eight. I'd seen the bus from Bathgate come and go from the stop near the flat, and there was no sign of the girls. They must be coming in from Edinburgh, I thought.

I walked into the living room to change the CD, and as I did I was aware of a car revving as it pulled away from the front of the flat. Seconds later my doorbell rang. I walked to the front door and looked through the peephole to see Vicky standing on the step. She was on her own. I pulled open the door and leaned forward to give her a kiss and a cuddle. I ushered her out of the freezing cold and into the warm hallway.

'Where's Leigh?' I asked.

'She couldn't make it. Her mum wouldn't let her come unless she drove her here, and Leigh wanted to travel with me, so they had a huge row, and Leigh decided she wasn't coming unless she could travel under her own steam. It's fine. I'm here now,' Vicky explained.

I must admit, I was a bit perturbed by the fact that Vicky had had to make the journey on her own but I was even more annoyed when I found out exactly how Vicky had travelled. She told me she'd caught a bus from Falkirk to Linlithgow, but when she got there her connecting bus to Livingston was either late or cancelled because of the bad weather. In desperation she'd called Uncle John and asked him if he knew the times of the buses to Livingston. He didn't, but he advised her to head home as the weather was so bad.

It was almost as if the fates were conspiring to stop Vicky getting to my flat; Leigh cancelling on her, her bus not turning up. But once Vicky's mind was made up to do something, she would do her utmost to see it through to the end. She would be damned if she wasn't going to complete the journey she'd fought so hard with Mum to allow her to make.

So, ever resourceful, Vicky found an alternative way to my flat. She befriended a girl she'd met at the bus stop who was also going to Livingston. They were both freezing cold and decided to share a taxi. I was angry with Vicky for getting in a taxi, even with another girl, and I told her so. I suppose Vicky was a typical teenager with no respect for danger – or authority – but I reminded her that she shouldn't be travelling with a stranger under any circumstances.

Then I proudly showed Vicky her room that I had scrimped and saved to decorate. She was my first house guest, and, showing her round, I felt very grown-up. My sister had come to visit me in *my* house. I left her alone to unpack, and I poured us both a glass of wine. We settled on the sofa and had a good old sisterly chat. She said she was so excited to visit me and had been looking forward to the weekend for days. Even when Leigh called off she said it made her more determined to get here, even if she had to travel alone.

We talked a lot that evening. I understood that she was seeing less of Dad and Christine, and she admitted to feeling restricted living at home with Mum and the twins; she felt that she couldn't breathe. Lee and Lindsay were typical six-year-olds and ran Mum ragged. I could tell that Vicky was glad of the escape this weekend – as if she was at last breaking free from the monotony and routine of family life.

Vicky confessed she was concerned about Mum's health and that the doctors had told her her blood pressure was high. I was worried too. On the few occasions I managed to visit Mum I suspected she had started drinking habitually and excessively. I even raised it with her once but she just dismissed it as having the odd social drink.

Mum's friend Jimmy was visiting a lot and the two of them would sit and drink and chat until the early hours of the morning, but Vicky's comments confirmed my suspicions that Mum was using alcohol as a crutch more and more. I promised myself I would broach the subject with Mum again soon.

Vicky and I chatted well into the night. It was the first

time since I had left home that we had spent so long in each other's company, and we covered every conceivable subject: our childhood; Mum and Dad; relationships; the future.

Vicky still hoped to work with animals and wanted to be a vet, although she realised she would have to start working harder at school. Her preliminary exams were approaching and she knew she had to get good grades before the real exams in the early summer.

It was exciting for me to hear Vicky talking so positively about her plans. She wasn't like many of the other 15-year-olds I knew whose only ambition was to find a man, get married and have children. Vicky was different. She wanted more for herself, and if God had been willing, I'm positive she would have found it.

*

The next day I let Vicky sleep in as I prepared breakfast. She appeared around mid-morning, breezing through the kitchen door with a huge smile on her face – just like she used to do when we were children.

Later that morning we caught the bus at the stop outside the flat and travelled the two miles to the Livingston Centre. As we walked from the bus terminus down through the underpass, I told Vicky our priority was to buy Mum's birthday present. I knew the style of earrings she wanted and we went into H. Samuel's and scoured the rows before selecting a pair. Then we went into the card shop and I bought Mum a birthday card.

This was the first time Vicky and I had gone shopping on our own. I suppose big sisters always look forward to the day they can take their younger sibling to the shops. As a child your little sister seems to do everything possible to annoy and embarrass you, but there comes a point in time when the childish squabbles end and a different, closer relationship develops.

On a whim, we decided to go into a clothes shop and dared each other to see who could try on the worst outfit. Within minutes it was just like being back in our bedroom at home when we had tried on Mum's clothes for fun. I wish I had had my camera with me as Vicky emerged from the changing room wearing a long layered rainbow-coloured gypsy dress teamed with a long-sleeved pussy bow blouse in emerald green, gold and yellow. She looked disgusting, but we both just howled with laughter.

We returned exhausted from our shopping trip. Vicky had said she would cook her speciality – spaghetti bolognese – for Scott and me. I sat at the kitchen table and smiled as I watched my sister busy herself with getting the ingredients ready for our special meal. I remember thinking we'd come a long way, Vicky and I, from the days when we were caught in the middle of our parents' separation.

Emotionally we'd both been through the mill with Mum and Dad, but as I watched my sister cooking for me in my own kitchen, I felt so proud that we had both turned out all right, despite the odds. It gave me a warm glow to consider my family now. My sister, happy and contented. My mum at last having moved on from the trauma of Dad leaving, and the twins, having been so young at the time, thankfully unscathed by the trauma of Mum and Dad's split.

As Vicky served up her meal I was the proudest big sister in the world.

We went out on the town that night. As she emerged from her bedroom, Vicky looked at least four years older than she was. She wore dark denim baggy jeans and a black halter-neck top. Vicky had a bob that was cut at her jawline, and with her hair done and make-up on she looked a proper young woman.

Vicky, Scott and I had a couple of drinks each and left the flat around 8.30 p.m. We walked across the road and caught the next bus into Livingston town centre. It was a five-minute walk from the bus terminus to the Waverley, and when we arrived the place was already busy.

Vicky and I chose an area with about six seats empty – enough room for my friends to join us when they arrived, and Scott went to the bar to order our drinks. He sat down as the DJ began to play his first record. Nobody got up to dance – it was far too early for that.

Chapter Five

Soon my friends arrived and I introduced Vicky to Marion, Sharron, Billy and Ian. It wasn't long before she was chatting away to them. As I sat and watched I was proud of the way she was handling herself. She exuded charm and confidence, at ease with my friends and even making them laugh out loud with her one-liners. Underneath the confident façade I knew she was quite shy, but she was brilliant at putting on a front. It was sheer bravado, but I could see she was loving every minute of it all. Her eyes were alive and she was relishing the attention she was getting.

The DJ put on the Sex Pistols' 'Anarchy in the UK' and I said to Vicky, 'Come on. Let's dance.'

'No chance,' she replied.

'Come on, I dare you,' I said. No sooner had the words left my lips than she was pulling me on to the dance floor. We were the only two dancing, but we didn't care. We just made complete fools of ourselves pogo-ing to the punk music.

To everyone's amusement Vicky bumped into me and sent me flying backwards. I nearly landed on my backside in front of the whole pub. She just stood there howling with laughter.

We staggered out of the pub at half past midnight – Scott, Vicky and I being among the last to leave. I thought about inviting some of my friends back to the flat for a party, but decided against it. It would be after 1 a.m. when we got to the flat, and I wanted to spend as much time as possible on my own with Vicky.

So Vicky, Scott and I walked home in the cold February air, reaching the flat 20 minutes later. Scott said he was off to bed. I didn't want the night to end so Vicky and I had a nightcap, and talked.

Vicky beamed as she said she'd had a fantastic time and said how much she'd liked my friends. She asked me if she could come back the following weekend, and this time bring one of her friends. I was delighted and told her she was welcome at any time. We chatted for ages until tiredness took over and one of us, I'm not sure who, nodded off.

I went to bed that night very happy. My sister was my best friend again, just as she was when we were children in Redding.

*

I woke next morning with a thumping headache, walked to the window and looked out to see thick snow blanketing the ground. I left Scott asleep and passed by Vicky's room. The door was shut tight. I guessed she was trying to sleep off a hangover as big as mine. I sat on the settee and put on the TV hoping it would distract me from the pain in my head.

Vicky surfaced around 11.30 a.m. I couldn't help laughing at her. She looked a mess with her normally perfect hair all over the place. She slumped into one of the armchairs. We discussed how she was going to get home later that afternoon.

Neither Scott nor I could drive, so Vicky needed to check the bus timetable for the Sunday times. I knew the best route was from Livingston to Bathgate, then a connecting bus to Falkirk. But there was a lot of snow on the ground, it was bitterly cold, and I wondered if the buses would be running regularly with the weather being so bad. As I stared out of the window, I was so concerned about the thought of Vicky getting public transport that I suggested she phone Dad to see if he would be able to come and collect her. She wasn't keen though so we decided, therefore, to make sure Vicky's bus was scheduled to run. As we walked to the phone box a few hundred yards from the flat the snow was falling hard. We phoned the bus station at Livingston, but there was no reply.

'What now?' said Vicky.

'Look, just phone Dad. He will be fine about picking you up,' I said. 'He'll realise the weather is terrible and he won't want you struggling to get home. He'll jump in the car and pick you up.'

But still Vicky wouldn't budge and said he would probably be busy.

'Then ask Uncle John,' I said almost out of desperation. She dialled our uncle's number, but there was nobody home.

Finally, probably because she could see the weather worsening even as we stood shivering in the phone box, she reluctantly agreed to phone Dad. She dialled the number, and it was answered almost immediately. I couldn't hear the voice on the other end of the line but I could tell that it wasn't good news. Vicky put down the receiver with a heavy sigh and a resigned look on her face. She told me that Christine had answered and when she'd asked to speak to Dad, Christine had replied that he was out and that they had plans for later that day.

'Try the bus station again,' I suggested.

She did and this time I could hear the phone being picked up at the other end. Hallelujah. The buses were running as normal despite the weather, and Vicky's bus – the 5 p.m. from Livingston to Bathgate – was scheduled to leave on time.

We walked back to the flat, our feet dragging through the snow, to kill some time before Vicky headed off. Around 20 minutes before her bus was due, Vicky gathered all her belongings together and stuffed them into her green and black sports holdall. I remember thinking how grown-up and smart she looked dressed in her blue flared jeans, maroon T-shirt, grey sweatshirt and black jacket.

I gave her Mum's birthday card and earrings that I'd wrapped, and she placed them carefully on the top of her bag. I looked out of the window. The snow had eased slightly, although it still looked bitterly cold outside. I pulled on my coat and said I would walk with her to the bus stop.

Vicky had gone rather quiet and wasn't her usual chatty self. I put it down to our late night, but she certainly seemed out of sorts. I'd already talked her through her journey back home, but as we walked along the road she asked me to go over it again. I told her that she would catch the 5 p.m. bus from Livingston to Bathgate which would take around 20 minutes. I said she should get off the bus at the last stop in Bathgate, and she should ask the driver to give her a signal when the stop was approaching if she wasn't confident about working it out herself. I told her the last stop was in George Place and she should walk down the road about five hundred yards to the next stop, which was opposite the police station in South Bridge Street. This was the stop the Falkirk bus left from, and it was due to arrive at 6.10 p.m., so she had plenty of time to get her connection.

I knew the route well, because these were the buses I caught when I went to visit Mum. I knew exactly how long each part of the journey should take and what type of bus normally travelled that route. I knew every twist and turn on the road. But Vicky was anxious, I could see it in her eyes. As we waited at the stop she asked me to go over the route with her again.

I suppose, looking back, it was a daunting trip for her to make: it was starting to get dark; she had to change buses; it was bitterly cold; she would be alone in a strange town waiting for a bus she wasn't even sure from which direction it was coming. I cursed the fact that I didn't drive, and it crossed my mind that maybe I should just get on the bus with her. I didn't want to baby Vicky by suggesting she couldn't manage on her own. I'm sure even if I had suggested making the journey with her she would have been against the idea; her pride wouldn't have allowed her to say yes. But there is not a day goes by that I don't wish I had insisted on travelling with her that night, that I could turn back the clock.

I looked at my watch. It was four minutes past five. The bus was late, but we weren't surprised as it had been snowing on and off for some hours now. It was inevitable that the buses would be a bit erratic because of the state of the roads. We were both absolutely freezing and we must have looked a pathetic pair as we waited.

'Vicky, maybe we should just forget about you going home tonight. Why don't you just stay with me for another night? You could go home in the morning,' I said.

'No, I've got school tomorrow. I have to get up early. We'll just wait a bit longer.'

It seems rather silly now, but she also said she wanted to get home because she was desperate to see the *Smash Hits* music awards on TV. Whatever the reason, nothing I could say was going to change her mind. I think she just simply wanted to get home because she had school the next day.

'Tell me again, Sharon. Where do I get the Falkirk bus?' she asked for what seemed like the tenth time.

I must admit my patience was beginning to wear thin. 'Are you not listening?' I snapped back. I immediately regretted being angry with her as she looked so much like a little girl lost.

Then we both saw the green SMT bus in the distance, and I smiled at Vicky as it slowly made its way towards us.

I put my arms around Vicky and gave her a great big squeeze telling her I loved her and that she should take care. I said I would see her next week and she said she would definitely come, and this time she would make sure Leigh came with her.

She bent down to pick up her sports bag as the bus slowed to a stop in front of us. The doors opened and I shouted to the driver to ask him if he could let Vicky know when he reached the last stop in Bathgate so she could get off. He shouted back that he would. I hoped it would put Vicky's mind at rest.

I told Vicky not to worry and gave her a kiss on the cheek, then watched as she paid the driver for her ticket. We just had time to shout goodbye to each other before the doors swished closed and the bus began to pull away.

The bus windows were grimy with dirt and salt from the roads, but I could just about make out Vicky taking the seat behind the driver. I gave her a final wave as the bus disappeared into the distance.

Vicky's obsession with her journey home showed me that despite her grown-up demeanour at the weekend, she still had a vulnerable side. I regret to this day not insisting that she stay the night, or not talking to Christine myself and demanding to speak to Dad; or even finding the money somehow to pay for the cost of a taxi – that I had been stronger and taken control of the situation. If I had done I wouldn't have waved my sister off on that bus. I would have looked after her properly, as a big sister should.

Instead I walked back to the flat through the deepening snow. I was so cold my hands and feet were numb. I consoled myself with the fact that at least Vicky was in a warm bus. Back at the flat I began tidying up, washing the breakfast dishes we'd used earlier.

Suddenly, as I was standing in the kitchen, I was struck by a sickening feeling that seemed to rise from the pit of my stomach. Something was wrong with Vicky. People talk about mothers getting a strange premonition when something happens to one of their children. A kind of sixth sense. That was how this felt. I had a real feeling that something wasn't right. I felt nauseous; that feeling you get when you are caught doing something wrong.

I told Scott how I felt, but he calmed me down, saying I was probably a bit paranoid because of the way Vicky was when we parted at the bus stop. He tried to reassure me that she knew where she was going and that she would be all right.

I couldn't call Mum because she didn't have a telephone, and it was in the days before mobile phones. I had no easy way of getting in touch so I couldn't do anything anyway. Scott suggested going out for the night. I didn't want to at first, but realised I would have to do something or I would drive myself mad.

We decided to go to Melville's Disco in the town centre, and by the time I'd tidied myself up, the terrible feeling had dissipated. Scott and I had a great night, leaving about midnight. I was so exhausted when I got home I went straight to bed.

Do I feel guilty about dismissing my fears about Vicky? Yes, I do. Perhaps if I'd followed my instincts in some way I could have done something. I'll never know now. Sadly, I think that by the time the doubts were in my head, her fate was probably already sealed.

*

It was just after 1 a.m. that I was aware of a noise echoing around the flat. In my sleepy state it didn't register at first. Then I realised it was a door buzzer. Thinking someone was trying to rouse a neighbour, I pulled the bedclothes up around me. Another buzz. Then another. I got out of bed and walked to the window, pulling the curtains apart slightly to see if I could see who was at the communal door below. Then I noticed the police car. My stomach churned as I opened the bedroom window. 'What is it?' I shouted.

'Sharon Hamilton? Is Vicky there with you?' one of the two officers replied.

I just stared at them, and that awful sickening feeling began to well in my stomach again. 'Is Vicky there?' they called again. I just couldn't answer.

I told Scott to go downstairs and let the officers in as I grabbed my dressing gown and wrapped it around me. My hands were shaking. All sort of thoughts were running through my head. What had happened? What had the police come to ask me? Deep down, I feared the worst and I knew exactly why they were here. The police don't knock on your door at one o'clock in the morning unless there is real cause for concern. I heard Scott opening the front door and letting the two officers in as I came down the stairs.

Chapter Five

I motioned to the officers – a man and a woman – to sit down, but they continued to stand. They said they were from the Livingston office. 'Sharon,' said the female officer. 'Your mum has called Falkirk Police and they have asked us to come and check whether Vicky is with you. Your mum is really worried about her. Is she here?'

I felt complete disbelief. Vicky hadn't made it home. I began to speak, but I seemed to be having trouble forming any words that made sense. Eventually I managed to blurt out: 'No, she's not here. I put her on the bus home myself.'

The officer explained that when Vicky didn't turn up home at the expected time, Mum's friend Jimmy had gone to Falkirk bus station to wait. When Vicky didn't get off the last bus, Jimmy went back and told Mum. Distraught with worry, she called the police.

I looked at Scott but he just sat there with a bewildered expression on his face. I told the police that Vicky had definitely caught the 5 p.m. bus to Bathgate, and explained her planned route home. My heart was pumping and all sorts of possibilities were springing to mind. I had to calm down and try to think rationally. There had to be an innocent explanation. If she wasn't at home then maybe she'd met a friend in Falkirk and ended up at a party or something. Yes, that was it. She's at a party and having such a good time that she's forgotten about the time. I knew I was trying to convince myself that this scenario was true. But how could Vicky be so selfish? Putting Mum through all this worry.

I was trying to grasp any feasible explanation, but inside I was scared. I knew this wasn't right. I also felt guilty. I was the last person in the family to see her. She was my responsibility, and now something had happened to her.

I told the police as much as I could about how Vicky was when she left, what she was wearing, what she was carrying. Before the officers left they told me to call them if she turned up back at the flat. I was worried sick and thought about trying to get a lift to Mum's. But what good would that do? Besides, I told myself, she's probably turned up safe and well by now. I decided to try and get some sleep and call one of Mum's neighbours later in the morning.

I went back to bed and lay in the dark thinking about Vicky, replaying the entire weekend in my mind, looking for clues. Apart from the journey, nothing else seemed to be troubling her. Maybe she'd had a row with Mum before she came to my flat and didn't want to tell me about it. Maybe there was something bothering her at school and she couldn't bring herself to let me know. There *had* to be a clue. There had to be a logical explanation. I drifted in and out of shallow sleep before the alarm went off at 7 a.m. I jumped up and dressed quickly before running down to the phone box to call Jim Davis, Mum's next-door neighbour. He was a good friend of the family's and didn't mind me using his phone to get a message to Mum if it was urgent. This *was* urgent. I dialled his number, and after just two rings, he answered. 'Hello, Jim. It's Sharon,' I said. 'Can I speak to my mum?'

'Sharon. Is Vicky with you?'

I felt my knees go weak. 'Is she not home yet?' I said. I could feel the tears welling in my eyes.

'No, and your mum is really upset.'

'I'm on my way. Tell Mum I'm on my way.'

I slammed down the receiver and ran across the road to the flat. Where is she? Where is Vicky? Where is my little sister? I thought. Something bad has happened. She would *never* have done this to Mum and me. I thought about poor Mum, pacing the floor, waiting for the door to open and for Vicky to come through. I had to get home as soon as possible.

I ran across the road to my neighbour Craig's flat, praying that I'd catch him before he left for work in Falkirk. When he answered the door I could have hugged him with relief. He saw the state I was in, and when I explained about Vicky he said he'd be ready to leave in a few minutes.

The journey to Falkirk seemed to take an age. I was willing Craig to put his foot down to get there quicker, and making any kind of small talk with him just seemed to make me more anxious. I was desperate to get home to see Mum and the twins, to help them as much as I could; to try and work out between us what might have happened to Vicky. There must be something that none of us had thought of. I assumed Mum had probably been awake all night; knowing her as a natural worrier, she'd just have crumbled under the strain.

I regretted not trying to get home after the police had called rather than going to bed. Mum must have been distraught, but I hadn't really been thinking rationally. As we got closer to Falkirk I racked my brain again to think what could have happened to Vicky; to try and have some sort of rational explanation to give to Mum to put her mind at ease. Could she have run away? Almost impossible, I thought. Firstly, she was not the type of girl to just go off on her own. Secondly, she had very little money on her.

Had the shoplifting incident been playing on her mind? She'd told me about it during the weekend, but she still seemed to find the whole episode funny, although she did admit she'd learned a lesson from it. Was she in more trouble and couldn't face telling me or Mum. Was she pregnant?

When you are in a desperate situation, you grasp at straws, and that was exactly what I was doing. Trying to console myself with the notion that there was a perfectly rational explanation. Truthfully I knew that this was so out of character for Vicky. She had never run away before, and she was such a positive character I didn't believe anything – any kind of trouble – would have prompted her to disappear.

I tried to put all other sinister explanations out of my head. I had to remain positive for my own sanity and for Mum and the twins.

Craig pulled up in front of Mum's house just before 8 a.m. I jumped out the car and ran straight across the front lawn, barging through the front door. 'Mum,' I shouted.

Jimmy stopped me in the hallway. He looked pale and serious. 'Your mum is with the doctor just now, Sharon.'

'A doctor. Why?' I said as I burst into the living room.

As I entered the room I saw the doctor leaning over Mum, about to give her an injection. Mum was sobbing uncontrollably, the tears running down her cheeks.

'I'm okay, doctor. Sharon is here now,' I heard her say.

The doctor began arguing with her, insisting on giving her the injection. Mum looked a mess. Her eyes were puffy and red with dark circles underneath. It looked as if she had been crying all night.

I told the doctor that Mum didn't need medication and not to give it to her. He backed away as I moved towards Mum. I glanced sideways and saw the twins sitting on the floor watching TV, thankfully oblivious – as six-year-olds can be – to the chaos that was going on around them.

I grabbed Mum and we hugged, her head nestling in my neck as she sobbed deeply. 'Vicky's been gone all night, Sharon. I haven't heard from her. Where is she? Something bad has happened, I just know it has.'

I tried to calm her down, and we sat together on the sofa. I tried to tell her that there would be a simple explanation and that Vicky would probably bound in the door at any minute, her usual lively self, demanding breakfast.

'She would never run off and leave us, Sharon. I just know she wouldn't. Something terrible has happened.'

'She'll be okay, Mum,' I said, as convincingly as I could. 'She'll be okay. We just have to stick together as a family and hope. We have to hope. It's all we've got.'

Chapter Six

MY LITTLE SISTER was missing. Gone. It was now a day since she disappeared and there were no clues why.

My hopes that she had met a friend in Falkirk and gone to stay with her after waving me goodbye last night or headed off to a party somewhere were gone. If she had done either of those things she would have been home by now. I knew there had to be something else. I had known it since that horrible moment in my kitchen when I got the overwhelming feeling that Vicky was in trouble.

Now I just felt helpless. If someone had taken Vicky then all I could hope for was that she was still alive and that she might manage to escape. Perhaps she was being kept prisoner nearby.

But, this was my sister, and it couldn't happen to us, the Hamilton family from Redding. This was real life. Things like this just didn't happen to an ordinary, working-class family like ours. We were just a simple family from a very anonymous little part of Scotland.

Apart from our parents' break-up nothing unusual ever happened to us. Things like this happened to other people who we saw on the evening news. Not us.

I sat in Mum's living room the morning after Vicky disappeared and my mind went into overdrive. I was desperately going through the events of the day before in my head, searching for the answer, searching for some clue in Vicky's demeanour, in something she said. But I could come up with nothing.

Mum was a wreck. She said she'd spent all night sitting up waiting for Vicky to come home. The police had taken as much information as possible from Mum and Jimmy before passing on details to their colleagues in Bathgate – these were the officers who arrived at my flat. The police reassured Mum they would do everything in their power to track down Vicky, but she was a complete mess. She just didn't know what to do or say.

I decided I had to take over, to take control of the situation as much as I could.

I told her it would be better if the twins went to school as normal, and she agreed. So I busied myself with getting them ready. The school was just five minutes down the road, and they were excited that their big sister was walking them there. I was grateful for the distraction, and Lee, Lindsay and I made our way out of the house and down the road to the school gates. I'm sure that the twins sensed something was wrong, but luckily they didn't ask any questions. I stopped at the gates, gave them both a hug and watched them run happily into the playground.

I did wonder if I should tell Lee and Lindsay's teachers about what was happening, but decided that there could be some developments by the end of the day. There was no point in worrying anyone else.

By the time I'd walked back to Mum's house, there was a police car parked outside. Maybe they've found Vicky, I thought as I rushed in the door, but they wanted to chat to me, to go over things again and to ask Mum who Vicky's friends were. They said they were planning to visit Vicky's school to interview her classmates.

Once the officers had gone I made Mum a snack. All she could do was smile and apologise for not being hungry. I urged her to eat, but she just couldn't face anything. My heart went out to her. She was shaking like a leaf. She'd had no food or drink for hours now and I told her she'd have to keep her strength up for the sake of the twins. She just stared at me, a vacant, helpless look.

I decided to call Uncle Ian, Mum's brother, to tell him what had happened. He said he would come round straight away and I was glad. Mum needed all the support she could get. He arrived within half an hour, and I could tell by his expression that he was shocked at the way Mum looked. But Ian and his wife Eleanor set about making tea and trying to cheer Mum up. I was so grateful they were there, as each hour that went by seemed to increase the tension in the house. Every knock at the door brought hope of news, but then disappointment.

After Ian and Eleanor left I tried to persuade Mum to get some sleep. She said her mind was racing too much. She kept asking me what had happened during the weekend; the same questions over and over again. She was trying to make sense of the situation, desperately seeking a clue in my answers. I tried to remember everything, to give Mum every detail possible.

At the end of the school day I left Mum and went to pick up the twins. When we got back Lee suddenly asked Mum where Vicky was. Mum looked at me, her eyes pleading for help. I picked Lee up and put him on my knee. I calmly told him that Vicky was with her friends having a good time and that she would probably be home soon. Thankfully, he seemed happy with my answer and jumped off my knee and ran off to play with his toys.

Every time the front door bell rang or opened, Mum jumped, hoping somehow it was Vicky on the other side. And each time I saw her eyes cloud over with disappointment. The police visited two or three times that day. On every occasion it was just to give us an update, but there was nothing positive. They said they had spoken to Vicky's schoolfriends, but none of them had heard from her. They told Mum that if Vicky hadn't turned up by the next day then the case would be handed over to CID, and would become an official criminal inquiry. Mum broke down when she heard this and began sobbing again. I tried to find the right words to console her, but couldn't. I was stunned, too. The situation seemed to get more unreal at every turn, and now we were being told detectives were getting involved. Somehow that news seemed to make everything that little bit more serious – as if it wasn't desperate enough. All I could do was hug Mum tight for what seemed the thousandth time.

In times of trouble throughout my life I have turned to and confided in my best friend Angela, and I really needed her now. As much as I tried to support Mum, I needed to speak to someone outside the immediate family; I needed to try and clear my head. She lived just ten minutes' walk away, and I set off knowing that Angela would put me straight.

When I arrived at her house her mum said Angela was out but was due back soon. I didn't want to explain to Angela's mum that Vicky was missing, or to ignore it and make small talk, so I set off to head back home. I'd only got about 100 yards along the road when I heard Angela's familiar voice behind me shouting my name. She was running towards me, as if she sensed there was something wrong. Before she reached me I burst into tears. Angela tried to calm me down and get me to speak to her, but I struggled to get the words out through my sobs. 'Vicky's missing,' I eventually blurted out. 'She's disappeared.' We hugged each other in the street before Angela turned me round and walked me back to her house. I was so grateful to her for being there for me. She listened as I told her about the events of the last couple of days and she asked me if there was anything she could do to help. But there wasn't, not unless she could wave a magic wand and bring Vicky home.

After I'd calmed down, with the help of a cup of tea, I felt strong enough to walk home and face Mum again. My chat with Angela had helped. I felt able to focus better. I had to concentrate on my family. I had to be strong for Mum, Lee and Lindsay. With Dad out of the house I was the one everyone relied on. I had to take control.

I also had to try and rid myself of this niggling thought that seemed to be haunting me – that maybe it was my fault that Vicky had gone missing. Maybe I should have spotted something or maybe I should have gone on that journey home with her. I had to stop feeling guilty and be positive – or I was going to drive myself mad.

During these first couple of days I'd phoned Dad a couple of times to keep him up to date with developments. He sounded genuinely worried about Vicky, but he never once offered to meet up or speak to Mum. His attitude baffled me. I would have thought it would have been possible for him to put his differences with Mum aside at a time like this and give some tangible support.

I realised I would have to go and see him face to face. I decided that if Vicky was still missing by the same time the following day I would pay him a visit.

What Mum needed now was some sleep. Jimmy said he would stay the night, and I agreed. At least he would be on hand if Mum needed him. By around 10 p.m. I noticed her eyes beginning to get heavy. She'd had a couple of drinks earlier in the evening, and the combination of tiredness and alcohol was beginning to have an effect on her. I fetched a blanket and tucked her into her favourite chair. I went upstairs to my old room to try and catch up on some sleep as well. Maybe tomorrow, I thought, God willing, we would have some good news.

I awoke early next morning around 6 a.m. The first person I thought of was Vicky. Irrational thoughts. Maybe she'd come home during the night and was here in the house with us. I sat up straight in my old single bed in the room Vicky and I once shared. I looked across at the other bed willing it to have Vicky in it. Part of me expected her to be lying there snoring her head off – just like she used to. My heart sank when I realised the bed hadn't been slept in. It was just as Vicky had left it the day she came to Livingston to visit me.

I lay in bed, my head in turmoil. Would the police have any news? How would Mum be today? I closed my eyes and prayed for news; a glimmer of hope.

I pulled on the same clothes I'd arrived at Mum's in the previous day and ran downstairs. I'd have to wake the twins soon to get them ready for school. Mum was still asleep in the living room – almost in the same position I'd left her in, and Jimmy was laid out on the settee. I closed the door quietly and went into the kitchen to make a cup of tea.

A few minutes later I heard the twins thundering downstairs; that woke Mum up and she began shouting for me.

'Have you heard anything?' she said, with a look of desperation on her face.

'No. Nothing,' I replied.

She immediately began busying herself with getting the twins' breakfast organised and getting them ready for school.

Neither of the twins asked about Vicky, although they must have found it strange that she hadn't appeared for breakfast as usual and she wasn't beside them getting prepared for school. They were only six years old, but children are very perceptive. They must have known something was wrong, but at the same time, and although they didn't know the reason, they saw how upset Mum was and didn't want to make her cry again by mentioning their sister.

I walked the twins down to school again, and when I returned there was a strange car parked outside Mum's house. I ran into the house and heard voices coming from the living room. As I walked in I was met by two men dressed in suits. They introduced themselves as CID officers from Central Scotland Police and said they were here to talk to me. Although we'd been warned that the CID were to become involved, it was still a shock to see them both standing there.

The officers told us what they planned to do that day. They wanted to take a full statement from me and Mum and then they wanted to speak to as many of Vicky's friends as possible. They also said they would speak to the press about putting an appeal in the papers asking for information from anyone who might have spotted Vicky on Sunday night.

All of a sudden things seemed to be moving very quickly. The officers were very professional and straight to the point. Mum looked shocked. Frankly, so was I. I just remember thinking how crazy it all was. One day I was plain Sharon Hamilton and my little sister had come to visit me for the weekend; the next I was catapulted into this unfamiliar world of the police and the media.

The two officers drove me from Mum's house to

Maddiston Police Station about three miles away. They put me in an interview room and gave me a cup of coffee. It was almost as if I had just dropped in for a chat. It all seemed so informal. They told me they had to take a full statement and I should do my best to remember every detail about the weekend. I was determined to help as much as I could and I tried to visualise all Vicky's movements from the moment she arrived on the Friday night. For eight full hours I relived my weekend with Vicky. Every single detail.

I suppose, looking back, I must have been a suspect, being the last member of her family to see her alive, but sitting in that room with the two officers I didn't feel as if I was under suspicion. I hoped there would be some clue in my recollections that would help solve the mystery of what had happened to Vicky.

The police wanted to hear everything; what we had talked about; who we had met; who Vicky had danced with – even what we'd had to drink. No detail was too trivial or unimportant.

Although the interview lasted eight hours it seemed to fly past. I think the officers must have set me off talking and just let me carry on as they furiously took notes all the while. During a break in proceedings, an idea struck me. I asked one of the detectives if it would be all right if I made some posters up and distributed them throughout

Bathgate. He said that if I felt it might help and make me feel I was doing something positive then he had no objections. I was delighted I was being allowed to do something practical; something tangible.

Before I left, the police gave me the first small clues about Vicky's movements after I had kissed her and waved her off on the bus. They said they had tracked down the driver of the Livingston to Bathgate bus who I had spoken to as Vicky got on. Even though she'd heard me ask him too, Vicky had asked the driver – Derek Brown – to let her know when the bus got to Bathgate. When he got there, everyone got off except Vicky, who remained seated directly behind him. He recalled saying to Vicky: 'This is your last stop.' He told the police: 'She got up and asked where she would get the Falkirk bus.' He said he told her exactly where she should wait for the connecting service.

The police said Vicky left the bus around 5.30 p.m. and walked the short distance to Valente's Fish and Chicken Bar in George Place. Shop assistant Linda Newman recalled Vicky being in the shop around 5.35 p.m. Vicky also asked her about where she should get the bus to Falkirk. Linda told the police: 'She was just a lassie going home. She asked for a bag of chips and then asked what time she got the bus and from where, and I told her.' Vicky was the only customer in the shop at the time.

After collecting her chips she walked across the road to the town's Steelyard Square, the central point in Bathgate where an old steelyard once stood in the early 1900s. It has remained relatively unchanged for decades and locals often gather at the old iron fountain in the square.

Mrs Newman told the police she glanced out of the shop window and saw Vicky eating her chips as she sat on a bench next to the phone box in the square. It was 5.45 p.m. 'The next time I looked up a few minutes later, the girl was gone,' she said.

But the police had also discovered that nobody had got on the Falkirk bus when it arrived in Bathgate. It appeared that Vicky had disappeared in an instant and the police were desperate to speak to anyone who saw her after Mrs Newman had last seen her on the bench.

One minute she was sitting on a bench in the middle of a town centre, the next she'd vanished. How could that have happened? I posed the question to the two officers. They just looked at me, clearly as mystified as I was.

The police said they also wanted to talk to Scott. I was a bit taken aback by this. Somehow, amidst all the chaos, I hadn't really given him much thought. I immediately felt guilty, thinking that I'd better give him a call as he'd be worried about me.

When the CID were finished with me they took me back to Mum's. I wanted to get started making posters of

Vicky and I had the perfect photograph of her in mind. I'd seen it in Mum's house. It was one of her school photographs. Vicky in uniform, smiling broadly for the camera. She looked as if she didn't have a care in the world. It had been taken six months earlier and the only difference between that picture and Vicky when she went missing was that her hair was auburn and not the jet black she'd dyed it before she came to visit me. But her distinctive bob hairstyle was the same. This photograph came to define my sister. It was the picture that was eventually flashed across the media, and it became the iconic image of the campaign to find her.

I told Mum about my poster plan and she thought it was a great idea. 'At least it's something positive we can do,' she said. As we discussed where we should put up the posters the doorbell rang. It was a reporter from the *Sun*. This was the first time I had ever dealt with – or even met – a newspaper reporter. I didn't realise then that I would meet countless journalists over the years, some of whom I would become friends with and some whom, quite frankly, I would wish to never meet again.

The reporter said he had heard about Vicky's disappearance and wanted some background information. I told him Mum was too upset to speak and that he should contact Falkirk Police Station for any information. As I moved to close the door he offered me his business card and said that if we changed our minds we should give him a call. I took the card and placed it in my back pocket.

Later I thought that if Mum wasn't up to speaking to the press, then maybe Dad would. I hadn't heard from him since my initial calls. I needed his support at this time and really wanted to talk to him about Vicky's disappearance and so resolved to see him the next day.

I carefully took Vicky's school photograph from the frame and placed it in a folder. I'd found a marker pen and some A4 paper, all I needed was a photocopier. I'd phoned round a few friends and explained what I wanted to do – to flood Bathgate with pictures of Vicky. Perhaps someone somewhere might have their memory jogged by her image staring out at them in the street. It was worth a shot and better than sitting at home worrying. Angela, Vicky's friend Claire and her friend Glen had agreed to come along. They were all desperate to do what they could to help. We all jumped into Glen's car and headed into Bathgate.

When we arrived around 6 p.m. it was already dark. We parked the car in the town centre and went in search of a shop with a photocopier. I was so desperate to get started that I began stopping people at random and showing them Vicky's photograph and asking if they had seen her. I must have stopped around a dozen people who all looked blankly at Vicky's picture. But I was fired with enthusiasm, and I would have asked everyone in the town if I could have.

We went into a petrol station in the main street where we thought they would have a photocopier. The assistant was a great help and we explained what we were doing and I showed her Vicky's photograph. Angela and I began devising our own missing person poster. It read MISSING in bold writing across the top of the A4 paper. I placed Vicky's school picture underneath, and below the picture we wrote: 'Last seen on Sunday at 5.30p.m., Bathgate area. Anyone with any information please contact Falkirk Police.' Then we put the police telephone number in bold across the bottom.

The assistant made 60 copies for us, and when we offered to pay she refused to take any money from us. She said she was just glad to help and hoped that we would find Vicky soon. She even gave us a roll of tape to stick the posters up with.

As we left the shop we stood and watched as she placed the first of our posters up on the window of the petrol station kiosk. That was the beginning of our campaign to find Vicky. I looked at her image staring back at me and thought, 'This is a dream. No, it's a nightmare. My sister's face on a missing person poster.'

I divided the posters up between the four of us and we set off along the streets of Bathgate. We taped them to literally anything that was standing still: bus shelters, lampposts, pub doors, litter bins. We also stopped people in the street as we passed them. The reaction was always the same; they hadn't seen Vicky and didn't recognise her from her picture.

It began pouring with rain, but still we carried on – until we'd put up every single poster. After two and a half hours we decided to head for home. I wanted to get back to Mum and the twins and to see if anything had happened while I had been out.

Our campaign had resulted in nothing positive. We hadn't met anybody who had seen Vicky. Perhaps I'd expected too much, but it was with a deepening sense of dejection that we made our way back to Falkirk.

But I felt angry too; angry because it was now 48 hours since Vicky had gone missing. Two whole days. Why was Vicky doing this to us? Was she scared of something that she couldn't face and had to run away? How selfish. I was consumed with anger and frustration. I also felt utter helplessness at being unable to find my sister and a determination not to fear the worst. Oh dear God, where could she be?

I arrived home wet and weary. Mum was still awake and the twins were tucked up in bed. Jimmy was trying to keep Mum's spirits up. When I walked into the house, although there were people in it, it felt strangely empty. It was as if death had popped its head in and then left again. The house was warm, but the dim lighting gave it a morbid hue. The TV flickered in the corner, but the volume was turned down.

It was as if Mum had been sitting waiting for a car to pull up outside. I don't know whether she was expecting the police or her youngest daughter to walk through the door. Sitting in her chair. Waiting. That was all she could do; all she was able to do.

Mum told me I looked tired and she offered to run me a bath. But all I wanted to do was sit quietly and think; to see if I could puzzle things out in my mind. I went upstairs to the room I used to share with Vicky. Terrible thoughts were running through my head about what had happened to her and I just kept pushing them away; trying to make the disappear as quickly as they had come.

You hear about children disappearing all the time. Most of them turn up fairly quickly. But then there are the unfortunate ones who don't turn up at all. The ones you hear about on the news. The appeals for information. The crying relatives pleading with faceless abductors to let their loved ones go; trying to appeal to their better nature. Tragic, tragic stories. Then, in most cases, they are found dead. How could anyone be so cruel as to kill a helpless child?

I sat and prayed to God that 15-year-old Vicky would not be one of those children.

I was surrounded by memories of her. I could visualise her lying in her bed; standing in front of the mirror combing her hair and putting on her make-up.

I closed my eyes and I could smell her smell. I could imagine her face. I could hear her laughter. With my head filled with good thoughts of Vicky, I found sleep.

*

The next day – Wednesday 13 February – I woke to find the twins asleep beside Mum. They only stirred as I entered the room. I told Mum to have an extra half-hour in bed and I got Lee and Lindsay ready for school.

It was increasingly obvious the twins knew that something was wrong. They couldn't understand why Vicky wasn't there, and Mum and I had to keep fobbing them off with white lies. They were both missing Vicky and all the while watching their mum and their big sister worrying and fretting. They were confused with the number of strange people coming and going in the house asking all kinds of questions. I was glad they were too young to fully understand. It was a blessing. Nothing, however, could have prepared any of us for what was to come – this was only the beginning.

Around mid-morning, the CID came back again. They didn't have any news, but they wanted to search Vicky's room. Mum told them she had already been through

Vicky's things looking for clues and had noticed that Vicky's bank account passbook was still in her room. She'd only opened the account a few weeks before, and the £10 she deposited was still there. To Mum this proved that Vicky had not run away. If she had, she figured, she would have taken her bankbook with her. Mum handed the book to the officers.

The two detectives then went into Vicky's room, removing items that they thought might be important, including her schoolbooks and diary.

There was clearly a great deal of police work going on behind the scenes. There was a dedicated squad of officers looking for Vicky from Central Scotland Police, who covered the area where Vicky and Mum lived, and they were working in conjunction with officers from Lothian and Borders, who were responsible for the Bathgate area where she went missing.

I now know that full-scale searches were made of wooded areas around Bathgate and police were also stopping and questioning motorists on a regular basis. In hindsight, it was impossible for police to phone us up every time they were doing something involved with the hunt. But for us sitting at home waiting for any snippet of information, it felt as if things were dragging along slowly.

Later that afternoon, I finally went to see Dad. I got the impression from things he said that he thought Vicky might be off on some teenage prank and would turn up eventually. I wonder if he, like Mum and me, felt in some way to blame for her disappearance, perhaps because he wasn't able to pick her up from Bathgate. Nevertheless, I was still upset that we hadn't seen him at Mum's house since Vicky went missing.

I was determined, however, that I would remain positive and constructive and keep him informed. After all he was Vicky's dad and the most important thing was to find Vicky. I wasn't going to let a family squabble jeopardise that.

After I'd filled him in he asked if there was anything he could do. I showed him the card the journalist from the *Sun* had given me. Dad thought it would be a good idea to try and generate some publicity and, to my surprise, he phoned the reporter straight away. The reporter said he was in the area and would be at Dad's house shortly. Dad then started to ask me questions about the weekend. He wanted to know every detail. It was as if a light had gone on in his head and he had just woken up to the fact that she had disappeared and that this might be really serious. He seemed as stressed as Mum and I had felt the last few days.

When the journalist began asking us questions about Vicky, Dad was in tears telling him about his fears and his last memory of Vicky.

It was the most emotional I had ever seen my father and yet I was still angry with him, resentments that just wouldn't go away about him leaving the family and my feelings of rejection. I rather reluctantly posed for a photograph beside Dad before the reporter was finished.

When I got home I told Mum that we'd put an appeal in the newspaper and that it was scheduled to appear the next day. She seemed pleased that, at long last, Dad seemed to be taking an interest. I couldn't help thinking that if the two of them could just talk then maybe they could help each other through this.

A couple of Vicky's friends arrived at Mum's house to see if there was any news. It was touching to see them there, showing their concern for Vicky and their support for her family. News of her disappearance was spreading around the school and they said rumours were rife about what had happened. The popular theory was that she'd run away, but her friends knew her and were convinced she wouldn't do such a thing. All her friends had been questioned by the police, but none of them was able to shine any light on what might have happened.

Later that night, there was a knock on the front door. 'I'll get it,' I said. Every arrival at the door filled me with dread as I feared the police had arrived with bad news. It was Mum's neighbour Mrs Cullen, who often took phone calls for us. 'Oh, Sharon. You are here. I thought it was you on the phone.' She looked confused. 'On the phone just now,' she said, gesturing towards her house where the door was wide open. 'You were asking to speak to your mum.'

'I don't understand,' I said.

'There's a girl on my phone asking to speak to your mum. I thought it was you, Sharon. I even said: "Okay, Sharon, I will go and get her." Sorry, it must be Vicky.'

I barged past Mrs Cullen, ran through the front garden, across the road and into her house where the phone lay off the hook. I picked it up. 'Hello,' I said. 'Hello.' The line was dead.

I was absolutely stunned. Mrs Cullen had known Vicky hadn't come home, but I don't think she realised the seriousness of the situation, or indeed that the police were involved.

Was that Vicky on the line? Had she managed to escape from somewhere and get to a phone? Was she phoning from somewhere she was hiding? Who else could it have been?

To this day I do not know whether it was Vicky who made the call or whether Mrs Cullen was in some way mistaken about the call. We told the police about it, but they never managed to trace it. But I have always been tormented by the thought that it was a cry for help from Vicky. I suppose now I'll never know.

That night Mum and I discussed what might have happened to Vicky. Some possibilities were almost too terrible to think about, but we had to meet this head on. I could see Mum was desperately trying to hold things together, but invariably she would dissolve into floods of tears. She was literally going out of her mind with worry. Mum hadn't left her house in three days. She just sat waiting for Vicky to come home.

I didn't sleep well that night. I heard every sound outside in the street even though Vicky's room – the one we used to share – was at the back of the house. I held my breath every time a car drove by. I visualised it slowing down and stopping outside the house. I could see Vicky getting out of it and the car driving off. My brain just wouldn't stop playing out this scenario in my head over and over again.

The next morning I dropped the twins off at school and went into the newsagents to buy a copy of the *Sun* to see if our interview was in it. It appeared on page 13 with the headline: 'Please give us back our Vicky alive' and a picture of Dad and me. It was a bit surreal to see myself in the newspaper and reading about my little sister, but it was something I would get used to in the ensuing years. When I showed it to Mum tears trickled down her face as she read it.

I hoped that someone reading it would have their

memory jogged by Vicky's picture and possibly remember seeing her in Bathgate that night. Maybe if she'd run away and was being helped by someone, that person would see how concerned her family was and make a phone call. Maybe if she was being held against her will, her abductor would find their conscience and let her go. Maybe someone out there would tell us something.

Later that day the police arrived and asked me if they could search my flat. I'd been expecting this. They drove me from Mum's house back to Livingston. Despite the fact I had nothing to hide, I felt nervous and my stomach was turning somersaults.

When we arrived at the flat, Scott was at work. The two officers immediately began asking questions. Where did Vicky sit? Where did she sleep? I gave them a tour of the flat, pointing out what they wanted to know. I watched as they stripped the bed where Vicky had slept, picking up stray hairs from the bedclothes. They asked if anyone had slept in the bed since Vicky, but no one had.

I sat down in the living room and watched as they systematically went from room to room, looking in every corner. I couldn't help thinking that three days ago my world had been normal and I had been living an ordinary life with my boyfriend in our little flat. Now I felt I was sitting in the middle of a crime scene.

It was Valentine's Day, and I thought maybe I should

stay in Livingston and see Scott when he returned from work. I got the impression from these early days of the investigation that Scott didn't want to get involved in the whole thing. Certainly I felt that he didn't offer me much support. I was surprised at his attitude, but perhaps he was just overwhelmed by events.

However, when the officers had finished their examination and offered me a lift back to Falkirk I didn't hesitate. Mum needed me more.

When the police dropped me off there was what looked like a battalion of media organisations in the street. My stomach churned. Why were they all here now? Had there been news about Vicky? I pulled myself together. She couldn't have been found because the officers who had dropped me off would have known. I burst into the living room to be met with a bank of film equipment and strange faces. The room was full of cameras, lights and cables.

The *Sun* article had obviously sparked people's interest and the story had gone to the top of the news agenda. Mum looked terrified. I motioned to her that that I wanted a quiet word with her. I knew Mum too well; she was such an obliging person it wouldn't have taken much for a persuasive journalist to convince her to do something she didn't really want to do. We went into the kitchen and I asked her if she was sure she wanted to go in front of the cameras when she was so vulnerable. I offered to deal with the press for her.

I could see she was petrified, but she said she could cope. She said it was something positive she could do to try and get Vicky home. 'I'll do whatever it takes,' she said.

I left Jimmy and Mum with the press and headed off to collect the twins from school. On the way back Lindsay spotted the TV vans outside the house. She asked who they were and I told her. She bowed her head. It was as if she realised the significance of their presence. As if she knew it was serious. After that Lindsay didn't mention Vicky's name for months. Whenever the police or the press were around and people were talking about Vicky, she left the room. Lee on the other hand started to ask lots of questions. Where was Vicky? When would she be home? Why was Mum so sad? The only question I could answer with complete honesty was that Mum was sad because she was missing Vicky and that she was worried about her.

When we got back into the house, one of the reporters asked if I could answer a few questions. I agreed and he asked me to sit beside Mum on the settee. When Mum was interviewed I heard her voice falter as she tried to speak. When it was my turn I felt a lump in my throat and the tears welling in my eyes. The ordeal of talking to a camera somehow seemed to magnify the situation – if that was possible. The stress of speaking about Vicky, knowing our words would be heard by millions, was huge. But somehow we got through it. For my part I just thought of Vicky alone somewhere and realised I had to get the message across that a schoolgirl had gone missing from the streets of Scotland, and someone somewhere must know something about it.

Over the next few days it was like a media circus at Mum's house. It seemed every newspaper, TV station and magazine wanted Mum and me to talk about Vicky; especially me, because I was the last person in the family to see her alive. All the press activity kept us busy during the day, but when the reporters and the camera crews had left we were alone again, waiting for news. But there was nothing from the police. The trail appeared to be going cold already.

Despite this, Vicky was all over the news. Front-page headlines. People were now stopping us in the street having recognised us from the newspapers and the news bulletins. The search for Vicky grew very quickly. There was huge police manpower involved in the operation to find her. There were two police forces working together – the first time Central Scotland and Lothian and Borders Police had worked jointly on an investigation of this magnitude.

Mum and I watched the news programmes and saw the

police carrying out fingertip searches throughout the Bathgate area. They searched fields and canals, back gardens, rubbish bins and garden sheds. The police had now made their own official posters and they seemed to be on every lamppost and building throughout Scotland. I was used to it now; seeing my sister's face staring back at me from every street corner.

Exactly a week after Vicky disappeared the police set up a road patrol in Bathgate town centre. They stopped every single car in the town that day and handed out leaflets with Vicky's picture on it. Vicky's face was everywhere. It was a constant reminder of the daily hell we were going through and Mum wasn't coping very well with the stress of it all.

One day the police called us and asked us to identify some clothing. I'm not sure where it came from, but it was an ordeal going along to the police station thinking that what we were about to see might be Vicky's clothes. We held each other's hands as we were shown a black bomber jacket similar to Vicky's. It was painful until we realised, with great relief, that the clothes were not hers.

Eventually it became obvious to the police that Mum was struggling healthwise and they gave her a contact number for Victim Support, an organisation to help victims of crime. It proved to be a turning point, albeit for a short time. When the lady volunteers from Victim

Support came to visit Mum they brought a basket of flowers. It was a simple gesture, but it was the first time I had seen Mum smile properly since Vicky disappeared.

Mum had also been assigned two CID Family Liaison Officers – one male and one female – by Lothian and Borders Police. Shona Livingston was to become a great friend and confidante to the family. She and Mum formed a real bond and Mum grew to confide in Shona a lot. Shona was one of a small group of officers we grew to trust and rely on and who would have walked to the ends of the earth to find Vicky.

The police also paid for Mum to have a phone installed in the house. It meant they didn't have to call out to the house every time they wanted to ask a simple question. It also meant Mum could phone Victim Support or the Samaritans whenever she wanted. And often she would. At home she had me to talk to, but perhaps I was too close to the situation and she needed to reach someone with a different perspective. This gave her the chance to talk to someone outside the immediate family, as I had with Angela.

The police were in constant touch with us – usually through Shona – and the newspapers were lapping up the story. Two weeks had come and gone, it seemed in an instant, and still there was nothing concrete to go on. No clues.

I didn't once see Dad at Mum's house during this period and don't know why he didn't visit, but I wish he had. The police searched his house, as with my house, which is normal procedure when someone goes missing – the relatives are checked out first. He didn't react well and gave an angry interview to the *Sun*, which ran with the screaming front-page headline: 'I didn't kill my girl'. As he hadn't warned us that he'd spoken to the paper it was a shock to see this in print

In the article Dad claimed he was being hounded by police who, he said, believed he had murdered Vicky. He said police had searched his house six times since Vicky had disappeared and had spent four days taking his car to pieces looking for clues. He told the newspaper: 'It doesn't take much intelligence to realise what they are looking for. I am sure they believe I killed her. But any thoughts that I could have done something to Vicky are absurd. I love Vicky more than anything else in the world, but the pressure I am under is making it even harder to cope with her disappearance.'

I was furious. Speaking out in that tone about a normal police procedure was going to do nothing for the family's relationship with the police. We needed their full cooperation and support if we were going to get a breakthrough in the hunt.

I called him straight away. He said the *Sun* had blown

his comments out of proportion. But I could tell by the tone of his voice that he was still livid.

He said the police were treating him like a suspect. I explained that the police were just doing what they had to do and that countless children had disappeared in the past, and on many occasions a family member was found to have been behind the abduction. I told him he just had to accept the situation, but he couldn't. I'd rarely heard him so upset and could see that these were unsettling times for all of us.

*

Four weeks of nothing. Then, in the most bizarre of circumstances, a breakthrough.

The clue came in the mail. I'd just walked down the stairs from my bedroom when the postman arrived with his morning delivery. As I bent down to pick up the bundle I noticed an official-looking letter addressed to Vicky.

It was a letter from Lothian and Borders Police lost property office to inform Vicky that her purse had been found on 20 February and had been handed in to them. The letter gave her details of how she could collect it.

Mum and I just stared at the note in disbelief. The same police force who were at that moment out looking for Vicky had sent a letter to her telling her she could collect her lost purse. How could this have happened? Vicky probably had the most 'famous' face and name in Scotland at that point but someone at the police lost property department had failed to make the connection between her and the computer-generated letter.

Mum immediately called Shona at Livingston Police Station and told her about the letter. I think she was just as shocked as us. This was the first clue to Vicky's disappearance and it had lain for days in a lost property department. Who knows who had handled it? There were probably dozens of sets of fingerprints on it already.

Mum was rightfully angry, but I managed to calm her down and reassure her that this could be a positive development. Little did I know that it would be the only real clue to Vicky's disappearance over the next 17 years.

Later that day the police arrived at the house with Vicky's purse wrapped in a polythene bag. It was spooky seeing it – the first tangible evidence of Vicky since 10 February. It contained her National Insurance card, a bus receipt from Livingston to Bathgate and a few pence, scraps of paper with some of her friends' phone numbers on them, and a picture of her friend's brother who was serving in the Navy.

The police then took my fingerprints along with Mum's to eliminate them from those that might be on the purse. The officers told us the purse had been found in the gutter at St Andrew's bus station in the centre of

Edinburgh. They said it looked as if it had just been thrown away. A full ten days after Vicky had disappeared someone found it and handed it in to the police.

But what did it mean? St Andrew's bus station is the main terminus in Edinburgh and from there you can travel directly to London. It wasn't on Vicky's route home – in fact it was in completely the opposite direction. Had Vicky run away and left her purse to throw people off the scent? Had someone taken Vicky and planted the purse at the bus station to lay a false trail?

The discovery of her purse opened up all sorts of possibilities and questions. But it was the first breakthrough we had had, and gave us hope that we might have taken a step on our journey to find my sister.

A week after the police had shown us Vicky's purse they told us they were planning a reconstruction of Vicky's last known movements in Bathgate the night she disappeared. The 'role' of Vicky was taken by Mary McGuigan, one of Lothian and Borders WPCs. She was dressed up in the same type of clothes that Vicky had worn when she left me. She was also given a holdall identical to Vicky's to carry. The police hoped that by the WPC being in Bathgate at the same time Vicky was last seen it would jog someone's memory.

Mum and I didn't want to go to Bathgate while the press were watching the reconstruction. Neither of us was ready to face it. So, instead, we watched it on the news. The footage showed 'Vicky' getting off the bus in Bathgate, walking a few yards into Valente's Chip Shop and ordering chips. Then she asked the assistant where she could catch the bus to Falkirk. She walked across the road to the area known as the Steelyard where she sat on a bench eating her take-away. The next scene was simply an empty bench. She had just vanished.

It was a strange feeling watching this whole scene played out on TV and it was simply awful watching a stranger 'playing' my sister with the whole thing being beamed to millions on television. Mum and I watched in silence. I glanced at her and she looked stunned. Broken. What was going through her head? She wasn't telling me much. She was bottling things up. She just sat there staring at the TV screen looking frail and very vulnerable.

Two days later, Mum and I found ourselves in front of the TV again as BBC's *Crimewatch* screened an appeal for information on Vicky. The police had jumped through hoops to get the appeal on air so quickly – just a month after Vicky disappeared – since the crimes featured are usually decided weeks in advance. This was prime-time television, and I know the police were particularly keen to get some nationwide airtime, and not just a Scottish programme, because of the theory that Vicky might have run off to London.

Mum and I watched as two pictures of Vicky were flashed up on screen, followed by an image of her purse. Maybe this time, I thought, we might just get a breakthrough. Someone somewhere in a remote corner of the UK might get in touch with that vital snippet of information.

I knew the police were pinning their hopes on getting something positive from the broadcast, and the initial signs were good. The 'update' programme later that night reported that they had received a large number of calls relating to Vicky's case. I was buoyed by this, and went to bed with renewed hope that the morning would bring news.

Detectives received 60 calls in total from viewers claiming to have information. Every single lead was followed. Every single one led to a dead end. I was devastated.

Our police liaison officers were disappointed too, and I sensed that they, perhaps for the first time, feared that Vicky might never come home. They avoided using the 'm' word, but they must have believed privately that my sister had indeed been murdered.

During these weeks, I was travelling back and forth between Mum's house and Livingston, but I had given up my job when Vicky disappeared and I was spending most of my time at Mum's. The search for Vicky was all-consuming, and I hadn't had a lot of time to think about

Scott either. Our relationship was deteriorating, and I knew within myself that I didn't want to be with him any more. It was nothing he had done; Mum needed me, and nothing was going to stop me being with her. I had made a commitment to put my private life on hold to help Mum search for Vicky.

So, three months after Vicky disappeared I moved out of our house for good and back to Mum's full-time. It felt like at least one weight had been lifted from my shoulders.

*

Over the 17 years we searched for Vicky we had our fair share of hoaxes and crank calls, but when it happened the first time, Mum and I were shocked to discover that there are people in the world who get their kicks by wallowing in others' misery.

The police received an anonymous call from a man claiming to have killed Vicky and dumped her body near a lay-by at the side of the main Bathgate to Falkirk road. Over 100 police officers from Lothian and Borders, Central Scotland and Strathclyde forces were involved in the search of a ten-mile area and 150 metres around every single lay-by, until they decided the call was a hoax.

I couldn't believe there were sick bastards out there who would want to waste police time and money, not to mention putting a family such as ours through more mental trauma.

But this was not the only hoax call police received – there were an extraordinarily high number in the early days of the inquiry. One young girl called a radio station claiming she was Vicky and that she wanted to pass a message on to her family saying she was living happily in London and that she wasn't coming home. The police seized a copy of the recording and asked me to listen to it. I knew immediately that it wasn't Vicky, her voice was nothing like my sister's.

We found ourselves in a catch-22 situation. We desperately needed the public's help, but inevitably if you appeal to a wider audience you are going to attract a fair number of cranks.

Around about this time Mum felt strong enough to carry out some more newspaper interviews. In one particular article in the *Daily Mail* she got very emotional and admitted for the first time in public that Vicky might be dead. 'I fear the worst,' she told the reporter. 'The best we can hope for now is that she is being held against her will, but is still alive.'

By coincidence Dad was also speaking to the newspapers, and he seemed to be coming to the same conclusion. He told the *Daily Express*: 'No matter what I think or what people tell me I should think, I still come back to the same conclusion. And that is that I'll never see Vicky alive again. I pray that I am wrong, but deep down I don't think I am.'

*

It was fast approaching Vicky's 16th birthday – 24 April. In Scotland, at the age of 16 you are regarded as an adult, and the police warned us that if they found Vicky after her birthday, and she had run away, then they couldn't force her to come home. This didn't bother Mum or me as we knew in our hearts Vicky hadn't run away. If by some chance she *was* living happily elsewhere and didn't want to come home, we would gladly trade that for simply knowing she was alive and well.

Vicky's birthday was a milestone Mum had been building up to, almost as if she were gathering her reserves of strength to cope with the occasion. She had bought Vicky a large wicker chair and on the morning of her birthday she placed it in the living room and set presents and cards from friends and relatives on top of it. There was a special card from the twins on which they had scrawled the word 'Vicky' on the front in coloured crayons. There were presents and cards from Mum's neighbours. There was even a giant card signed by 50 of Vicky's classmates at Graeme High School. Mum draped a huge pink bow and ribbon over the chair. It looked beautiful.

Mum remained strong for most of the day, but every time the phone or the doorbell rang, she jumped. She managed to keep herself together when two neighbours from a local charity group called with two bouquets of flowers but after they'd gone she simply dissolved into tears.

Vicky's presents sat untouched in the living room all day. In fact, they remained in the same place for months before Mum could summon the strength to put them away.

By evening, Mum and I were both exhausted with all the comings and goings in the house. As I kissed her goodnight before heading for bed, Mum looked broken. She had so desperately hoped that Vicky would come home that day – the day she would have become an adult; if Vicky had been alive and well, that day was the day she would have got in touch.

I suppose it was inevitable, but over the next few weeks things quietened down considerably. Our liaison officers conceded that new leads were scarce, although there was still a dedicated squad of officers working solely on Vicky's case.

I decided I had to try and get back to work for the sake of my own sanity. By a strange quirk of fate I found a job in Bathgate, the town where Vicky went missing. My friend's father owned a bar there and was looking for staff. I'm a great believer in fate, and it was while working there that fate got involved. I was immediately attracted to Les Brown, the pub's resident DJ, and he would become my emotional rock – and my husband.

At first I found it strange working so close to where Vicky was last seen, and she was constantly on my mind. I looked at everyone I served and wondered if they'd seen Vicky that night or seen someone offering her a lift.

While I kept busy, I continued to try and think of ways of keeping Vicky's name in the news, but it was difficult. The local press were fantastic and carried stories regularly, but the national papers weren't interested unless there had been a development or it was a significant date such as Vicky's birthday.

It was during the quiet times in the inquiry – and God knows there were plenty of those – that it was imperative to stay strong and focused. I especially endeavoured to be positive in front of Mum.

There were occasional 'sightings' from all parts of the country – from Inverness to London – but every time our hopes were raised, they were dashed just as quickly. It was disheartening, and it was easy to become blasé about these so-called sightings.

But when you are desperate for information, you will grasp anything, even from the most unlikely – and unreliable – of sources. Mum and I had a number of encounters with psychics and clairvoyants over the years we were looking for Vicky, but none more upsetting than our first meeting with Scottish psychic Ann Anderson.

One morning, about four months after Vicky disappeared, Mum's doorbell rang at around 11 a.m. I opened the door to find two women on the doorstep, one aged about 50, the other slightly younger. The older woman appeared nervous and asked to speak to Mum.

She looked Mum straight in the eye and said: 'Your daughter is dead.'

Mum gasped in shock and asked: 'Who are you?'

The woman introduced herself as Ann Anderson and said she was a psychic. Her friend was a freelance journalist. She asked if she could come in. I think Mum was so shocked by what Ann Anderson had said that the pair of them were halfway into the house before she realised it. Once inside Ann began to tell Mum what she believed had happened to Vicky. Mum and I couldn't believe what we were hearing, but something, I suppose curiosity, stopped us kicking the pair of them out.

Ann Anderson claimed Vicky had been abducted and killed and that her body would be found near Beecraigs Country Park, about two miles from Bathgate. Mum and I were very upset when we heard this, but in a strange way we were drawn to this woman and the shocking story she was telling us.

Then she said: 'I've found one of Vicky's earrings.'

Mum and I looked at each other in complete shock.

'Where? Have you told the police?' I demanded.

'Yes, I've told the police. I'm working with them on the case,' she replied.

Then, almost as quickly as she'd descended upon us,

she was off again, muttering that she had to leave immediately. After she'd gone, Mum and I simply didn't know what to say to each other. We were both stunned.

'I'm calling the police,' said Mum. 'I need to know if this woman is worth listening to or not.' CID said they had heard of Ann Anderson, but were not officially working with any psychics, despite a few of them making contact about Vicky's case. 'She claims she's found Vicky's earring,' I heard Mum say. 'She might be worth checking out.'

The following day Ann Anderson's claims about Vicky were all over the *Sun* newspaper. She repeated her claim that Vicky's body was hidden near Bathgate – and that she would lead the police to the spot next week. Mum was horrified and called the police again to complain and to ask them to establish once and for all if any of Ann Anderson's claims were true.

The police later told us that they did search the area she had outlined and found nothing. They also visited her in her house in Fife and confronted her about the earring she claimed was Vicky's. She immediately backtracked and claimed she was mistaken and that the earring she had didn't belong to Vicky after all.

Feeling angry and betrayed, Mum vowed never to speak to anyone claiming to be a psychic or clairvoyant from that day on.

*

Chapter Six

By six months after Vicky's disappearance, every day followed a similar pattern. I would drag myself out of bed, help Mum with the twins before they went to school, and we'd hope that the day would bring some news of Vicky. On the days I was working in the pub I'd head off to Bathgate around teatime.

It is fair to say that as each day passed our hopes faded just that little bit more.

Still Dad never came to see us. I was hurt and upset. He occasionally appeared in the newspapers but otherwise I didn't know how involved he was in the hunt, whether he was talking to the police or not. My dad's brother John was Mum's only real link with Dad, and he would often pop in to see how we were doing. She grew to lean on John for advice, and one day she took him aside and asked him if he would he would be willing to be the person who identified Vicky if her body was found. John looked at her and nodded his head. Mum was relieved. There was no way she could have done it, and really it should have been Dad she asked. But she said that he didn't seem to want anything to do with her and the family and so she would have nothing to do with him.

I was beginning to worry more and more about Mum's health. She hardly seemed to eat anything and always said she had little appetite. All she wanted to do was talk about Vicky and speak to the police to find out if there had been any new information. We'd been worried about her drinking before, but I noticed she had started drinking more and more. I raised this with her, but she immediately dismissed any suggestion that there was a problem.

She would descend into black moods and it was hard on the family trying to deal with her some days. But it was hard to criticise her. All I could do was sympathise.

I'd also begun to rely more and more on Les. We were getting on really well and I decided it was time to introduce him to Mum. I wasn't sure how she was going to react because I was just 20 and Les was 35. The age difference didn't matter to me. What was more important was that he was giving me the support my father should have been providing, and now, looking back, Les was the father figure I craved. When Les came to Mum's house there was no doubt they got on well, but after he'd left she warned me that she thought Les was too old for me. She told me it was a phase I was going through and the relationship would soon fizzle out. I was very hurt at the time, but she didn't go any further and try and stop me seeing Les. She seemed to accept I was happy with him.

*

In September the twins celebrated their seventh birthdays; another very difficult day for everyone. I could tell Mum was dreading it, but she did her best to make it special for them.

Mum bought them a big cake and presents and fussed over them all day. Again, the press came to the house and took pictures. It was another excuse to get Vicky's picture in the papers. It was seven months since Vicky had disappeared and it was vital that we seized every opportunity to highlight the case.

Two days after the stories appeared in the newspapers a man knocked on Mum's door. He said his name was Charlie and he was from Glasgow. He was a small, middle-aged man, smartly dressed in a brown suit and tie. I thought he looked a bit eccentric, especially when I spotted he was wearing a Laurel and Hardy badge in his lapel. He said he had read about the twins' birthday and he wanted to give them a present. Mum – ever the trusting soul – invited him in and made him a cup of tea. He gave the twins £10 each despite Mum's protests, stayed for around an hour and then left to catch his train back to Glasgow.

A couple of days later Mum received a letter from Charlie. He claimed to know of a gang in Glasgow who had abducted Vicky and planned to sell her as a sex slave. He said she was being held in an abandoned factory warehouse somewhere in the city. He warned Mum not to contact the police or the gang would kill Vicky.

Mum was distraught, and was even more upset that she'd invited him into her home. There was an address on the letter, which we both thought was odd. I persuaded

Mum that she had to tell the police, and two officers arrived very quickly and took away the note. I think deep down Mum knew it was another hoax, but we couldn't dismiss a potential lead, no matter how unlikely.

We didn't have to wait long. Within hours the police contacted us and told us Charlie was a man who lived in a fantasy world and was obsessed with Laurel and Hardy. All his claims were bogus and the police had warned him never to bother us again.

The incident did nothing to improve Mum's state of mind or well-being and she began to feel unsafe in her own house. The police tried to reassure her that this was an isolated incident, but arranged for a locksmith to fit bolts to the front and back doors. Our house ended up as secure as Fort Knox, but at least it put Mum's mind at ease. I, on the other hand, was very shaken by this episode. How could anyone be so cruel? Couldn't they try and empathise with what we were going through as a family?

Fortunately, these feelings faded as I began spending more and more time with Les, and after working at the pub I would often stay over at his house. If I planned to stay with Les, Mum always made me phone her to let her know.

Then, out of the blue, Les proposed. I couldn't believe I had found happiness at a time when I seemed to spend weeks on end being sad. Mum, however, didn't see it that way. She was still adamant that he was too old for me.

Maybe she was being protective. Maybe she didn't want to 'lose' another daughter, albeit under completely different circumstances. She told me she thought marriage was the wrong thing for me and refused to give me her blessing. She even said she wouldn't go to my engagement party.

I didn't push it with her. She had enough on her plate and I knew a huge row was the last thing we both needed. I just consoled myself with the belief that eventually she would come round when she saw how happy and contented I was.

Dad on the other hand seemed quite delighted I was planning to marry. He told me that as long as I was happy, he was happy. Maybe he was most pleased at the thought of another man taking care of me – one less responsibility for him, not that he'd shown a great deal of that over the years.

For me, at 20 years old, I was determined that I had to start getting on with my life. I was just as driven as ever to find Vicky, but Les had offered me an opportunity to move forward, and I was determined I was going to grasp it.

*

Thousands of people go missing in Britain every year, many of them children and, because of our situation, it was inevitable we became more and more aware of this – growing – problem throughout the UK.

Mum was in touch with the Missing Persons Helpline on a regular basis – especially if she was having a really bad day. She was even on first-name terms with many of the volunteers who manned the phone lines. During one of these conversations Mum mentioned that she really admired Diana Lamplugh, whose daughter Suzy, a London estate agent, had gone missing in 1986, five years before Vicky. Diana Lamplugh had set up the Suzy Lamplugh Trust to help the families of other missing people and highlight safety rules for women and Victim Support said they would put Mum in touch with the Trust. Before long Mum was chatting on the phone with Diana on a regular basis.

I could see her heart-to-hearts with Diana were making a difference to Mum. Just being able to chat with another woman who had gone through a similar experience must have helped. Also Diana was able to give Mum the strength to cope as she had survived five years of her daughter being missing.

It wasn't long before Mum had arranged to travel to London to meet up with Diana. It gave her something to look forward to, and she was desperate to meet this brave woman face to face. So, in October Mum travelled to Diana's home near Richmond. When Diana answered her door she greeted Mum like an old friend, throwing her arms around her and giving her a warm welcome.

Diana showed Mum pictures of Suzy as a child and relived the day she found out she'd gone missing after going to meet a client called 'Mr Kipper' at an empty house in London her company had been trying to sell. Mum told the story of Vicky's last weekend with me in Bathgate and outlined her last fateful journey by bus to Bathgate.

It was an emotional meeting between two women with a common tragic bond.

Diana, who had long accepted that her daughter was no longer alive, asked Mum, 'What do you think has happened to Vicky?'

Mum paused before whispering, 'The honest answer is I think she is dead too.'

But Diana gave Mum hope for the future and the will to cope with the enormous pressures she would continue to endure. She told Mum: 'I dread birthdays and Christmas. I don't buy presents for Suzy, but it's very tough. I howl every Christmas.

'But you have just got to make yourself go on. We have no choice. Like me, you will probably look at other girls in the street and ask: "Why *my* daughter?" But life isn't fair to some of us. We know we will never see Suzy again – but we'll keep hoping and praying that Vicky comes home.'

When Mum returned home she looked and sounded more positive. She was thrilled to bits about meeting Diana – Mum said she was a very brave and kind woman – and found the whole experience very emotional. I got the impression that Diana had given Mum new strength to go on with the campaign. Mum was even so inspired by Diana and the Trust she'd established to help other families that she said she wanted to explore the possibility of setting up a similar government-backed helpline in Scotland.

Mum made an appointment with our local MP Michael Connarty to see him at his weekly surgery and she explained what she wanted to do. He was very enthusiastic and charming, but two weeks after our meeting Mum received a letter from him explaining that the government's view was that one helpline for the whole of the UK was sufficient, and there was no need for a separate Scottish operation. If Mum wanted to do this she would have to fund it herself.

Mum was disappointed, but realised she could never afford to establish something like this without financial help. She reluctantly gave up on the idea, but I was angry. From a personal point of view, the way I saw it was that it wouldn't have cost the government much to set up a Scottish hotline, and, more importantly for me, it would have given Mum a much-needed focus.

*

We were all dreading our first Christmas without Vicky. Mum and I discussed buying presents for her as we had done on her birthday, but she decided instead to put some money aside, just in case she came home.

Mum gave an interview to the local newspaper, the

Falkirk Herald, in which she said: 'Vicky always pushed me to put the tree up early. She loved Christmas. She bought the cards and wrapped most of the presents for me.

'It's hard to think of Christmas without her. She was the life and soul of the party.

'Vicky has a building society account. We're thinking of putting some money in that. If, God willing, Vicky comes home, she can withdraw the money herself.'

Christmas Day came and went, and it was one of the worst days of my life. We tried to make it as upbeat and happy as possible for the twins, but Mum kept leaving the living room to cry alone. I felt helpless. I couldn't do anything to take away her pain and suffering.

I didn't fully appreciate it back then, but facing days like Christmas, anniversaries and birthdays was slowly killing Mum. It was a slow process, but my mum was literally dying inside.

There were some positives around this time. I turned 21 a month after Christmas, but I didn't want a fuss as I didn't think it was appropriate to celebrate my birthday when we were no closer to finding my little sister.

Les offered to cook me a meal and then we planned to go and visit Mum. On the way to Redding I went to see Dad. He was lounging around in the living room with Christine. He wished me a happy birthday and handed me a card. He said he wanted to get me something nice for my 21st and asked what I would like. I told him Les had bought me a beautiful gold charm bracelet and I asked him if he would mind buying me a coffee bean charm to hang on it. He promised he would and we left for Mum's house.

On the way Les suggested stopping off at the pub just down the road for a celebratory drink – just the two of us. As we walked into the lounge I found myself surrounded by friends and relatives all singing 'Happy Birthday' to me. Mum and Les had organised a surprise party for me. But the biggest surprise of all was that in the corner of the pub sat Dad and Christine. I couldn't believe it. Here were Dad, Christine, Mum, me and the twins all together under one roof. I'd never have thought it possible. Mum and Dad managed to avoid each other all night, and they had put their differences aside for me. It was a fantastic evening, and one I will never, ever forget.

I never did receive my coffee bean charm from Dad. It made me very sad, not because he didn't buy me anything, but because he'd made a promise to get it, and he'd forgotten. Or he just hadn't bothered. But what mattered is that everyone made the effort and, for one precious night, we put all our troubles behind us and had fun. We'd all been through so much.

*

Mum and I realised there would be immense press interest in the lead-up to 10 February – the anniversary of Vicky going missing – but nothing could have prepared us for the deluge of reporters, camera crews and police officers who descended on our home.

It had been a year in which, apart from the discovery of Vicky's purse, there were no real hard clues to explain what had happened to her on that night.

The police were obviously keen to rekindle interest in the case and printed up some new posters using a photograph that the public had never seen. I smiled when I saw the picture they chose, because Vicky would have been so angry. It was taken the Christmas before she went missing, but she wasn't exactly looking her best. She had just woken up on Christmas morning, and I took her picture as she looked all dishevelled, dressed in a pink dressing gown without any make-up on. I remember thinking she would freak if she knew we were planning to beam this photo of her all around the UK. But we also knew that what was important was to kick-start the campaign to find her, and if a new recent picture of Vicky would do the trick then we had to try it.

On the day of the anniversary, the police took Mum to Bathgate to show her the incident room – the HQ from where the Vicky Hamilton inquiry was being run. They had invited the press along too and had also set up a police incident caravan in the middle of Bathgate Main Street. Dad had turned up too and when I look back at the press cuttings it was quite laughable seeing Mum and Dad walking down the street together, yet both seeming to purposefully keep their distance. Police then escorted them both towards the caravan, where the press were waiting outside. As soon as their cameras started clicking and the reporters began asking questions Mum was so overcome by the emotion of the occasion that she broke down in tears, right there in the middle of the street.

The police also staged another exercise in the centre of the town by retracing Vicky's last footsteps again. They questioned passengers on the same bus route at exactly the same time Vicky caught the bus from Livingston to Bathgate, and they interviewed drinkers in local pubs and handed out leaflets to hundreds of passing motorists.

But, sadly, all the effort was for nothing. There were no new leads. Absolutely nothing. I think this was the final straw for Mum. It had taken a great effort for her to participate in the police's new appeal, and now with nothing to show for it, she became a virtual recluse.

Chapter Seven

MUM HARDLY EVER went out over the following months. She hated the fact that people recognised her and pitied her. The only regular contact she had was Jimmy, who was very kind to her, often staying over to keep her company.

I was determined my relationship with Les would not suffer, but Mum needed me around and I tried to see her as much as possible. One day, not long before Christmas, when I came home to see how Mum was doing Jimmy said she was upstairs having a bath and would be down soon. But when she walked though the door I was shocked. It sounds cruel but for all the world she looked like the Michelin Man. She was bloated from her waist down.

She'd been complaining of swollen ankles for weeks, and eventually after a lot of nagging, she had been to the doctor who told her she wasn't doing enough exercise. Mum dismissed this advice because she spent most of the day burning up calories running after the twins. When I saw her, I told her she should go back to the doctor and ask about the swelling again, because it was definitely spreading.

She went back the following week and the same doctor told her to relax and put her feet up. You only had to look at Mum to realise there was something terribly wrong. I wasn't happy with the diagnosis and demanded she visit another doctor for a second opinion. This doctor took one look at her and said he wanted her to see a specialist at Falkirk Royal Infirmary. At last, someone was taking this seriously.

Her appointment came through and I went with her to see the specialist. I sat in the waiting area for 40 minutes before a doctor came out to speak to me. He took me away from where other people were sitting and said in a quiet, measured voice that he wanted to admit her to a ward there and then for further tests.

My immediate reaction was that she couldn't go into hospital now. By this time it was just a few days before Christmas and she had two eight-year-old children at home who needed her. He reluctantly agreed she could go home for Christmas on the understanding that she returned on 27 December.

I asked him what was wrong with Mum, but he couldn't or wouldn't say. I'm not sure which. So I was in the dark, and so, it turned out, was Mum. I told Mum we had to put this to the back of our minds and concentrate on giving the twins the best Christmas possible. I said she had to remain positive and that whatever was wrong with her would be fixed just after Christmas. All the time my mind was going into overdrive. What if she wasn't okay? Would she be in hospital for weeks? Months? What about the twins?

Could this family deal with any more tragedy than it had already? Surely fate would deal us a kinder hand.

I invited Mum and the twins to our home for Christmas dinner. It was a small one-bedroom flat but the living area was large and had plenty of room for us all to sit down and enjoy our meal.

Les cooked chicken instead of turkey because it was Mum's favourite and I bought her non-alcoholic wine to go with her meal. Even in the couple of days since she'd been to the hospital I could see her deteriorating before my eyes. She was not very mobile and she found it difficult to get comfortable. She couldn't get her shoes on her swollen feet and was forced to wear slippers all the time. She struggled to get up and down from the settee.

I did my best to ensure she was as comfortable as possible, raising her badly swollen legs onto a footstool. She watched us all dancing around the living room to Christmas songs and she did her best to smile, but I could tell she was in terrible pain.

Mum had spoiled the twins with their Christmas presents, buying them a computer games console and bicycles. I don't know where she got the extra money from, but she had made this Christmas extra special for them.

Looking back, I often wonder if Mum knew that if she went into hospital she might never come out again. I think she knew this might be her last Christmas with her family.

Mum spent Boxing Day at her own house with Jimmy, and Les and I visited them. We all enjoyed a nice quiet day lounging around watching television and playing with the twins. The next day Mum would be going back to hospital for tests but the subject was not raised until she leaned over late in the day and asked me to look after the twins while she was in. 'It will just be for a couple of days,' she said.

But after two days it became clear that Mum's stay would be longer. I took the twins to visit her, but she told me not to bring them again because she didn't like them to see her in hospital.

I asked Mum what was wrong with her, but she said she didn't know yet. I even asked the staff nurse for some information, but all she would say was: 'Mrs Hamilton doesn't want anyone to know.' This just made me worry even more, but Mum was saying nothing. All I could do was continue to visit her and look after the twins. New Year was just around the corner, but I couldn't see Mum getting home in time.

Hogmanay, usually a time of great celebration in Scotland, was a muted affair in our house. Mum was still in hospital and I still did not know what was wrong with her. My upstairs neighbours came down to 'see in' the New Year with us. I wasn't much in the mood, but after a couple of drinks I began to relax.

The twins were tucked up safely in bed when, around 11 p.m., my telephone rang. On the other end of the line was a nurse from Falkirk Royal. She said Mum was having difficulty breathing and that the doctors had moved her to the intensive care unit. They said I could come and visit her anytime I wanted.

I put the phone down with the nurse's 'invitation' still bouncing around my head. There was a sort of finality in her statement. Why was she saying we could visit at any time? Why was she phoning me an hour before midnight on Hogmanay?

I needed to go and see Mum straight away. Our neighbours agreed to stay in the flat and look after the twins, and Les and I headed for Falkirk. When we arrived at the intensive care unit, a doctor motioned for me to go into a side room. He explained that the fluid that had been building up in her body had now reached her lungs. He said he was doing what he could to drain them, but she had been placed on a life-support machine to help her breathe.

He warned me that Mum was surrounded by a bank of machines and had been connected to a number of wires and tubes, but that I wasn't to be alarmed by the sight of her. Even with this warning, when I stepped inside the single room to see her lying, eyes closed and helpless, I immediately burst into tears. She appeared lifeless and had breathing apparatus coming from her mouth and a variety of drips going in and out of her body. Her skin had a horrible grey pallor and her hair, which she was so proud of, seemed to have lost its sheen. All Les could do was hug me. My mum was being kept alive by machines and there was nothing I could do to.

The next three days seemed to pass in a blink. I was continuously in and out of hospital visiting Mum. I'd told Mum's brothers and sisters and they visited too. I could see during every visit how shocked they all looked as they saw Mum lying there hooked up to myriad machines. But there was no change in Mum's condition. She appeared to be in a coma-like state, and she never gave a flicker of recognition when I talked to her. There was just nothing.

I went to visit Dad to tell him about Mum. When I arrived, I realised he had been drinking and I don't think he really understood what I was telling him. All he could do was give me a big drunken hug. I really needed my dad right then ... I had Les to support me, but it wasn't the same.

When I left him it just made me more determined and sure of what I had to do; I had to try and hold this family together as best I could. I had to be strong for the twins, who were unable to understand why their mum was in hospital for so long.

Still the staff at the hospital refused to tell me anything. My requests for information were met with answers designed to brush me off. I can only think that Mum had instructed the staff to keep details of her illness to a minimum to try and protect the family. That would have been typical of Mum; selfless and compassionate.

In the end I stopped pestering the staff for information and accepted that they were doing everything they could for her. I concentrated on keeping things together for the twins while trying to put in the odd shift at the bar. Looking back I'm not sure where I found the strength.

On the third day of Mum being in intensive care I arrived at the hospital to be told by a doctor that Mum was awake and had begun pulling the tubes and wires from her body. He said staff had had to sedate her to calm her down. Then the doctor revealed the first clue to the root of Mum's illness: her body was going through withdrawal symptoms and was crying out for alcohol. So there it was. I knew Mum had been drinking more than usual since Vicky disappeared, but she must have had a bigger problem than I realised. I don't know how she had managed to hide it so well.

I was heartbroken, thinking I should have forced the issue when I had confronted her earlier about her drinking. I should have done more. I should have been with her more. But it was Mum's way of coping with stress – to reach for the bottle. I just didn't realise how much she had been doing it.

Now it might be too late.

The doctor told me that Mum's lungs were still struggling to cope and allow her to breathe unaided, so she was still on a ventilator. He also explained that there were further complications with Mum's kidney and liver functions. He pointed out two small blips on Mum's bedside monitor. These were her lungs, and although they were functioning, they were very weak.

After days of being refused information about Mum I was now being bombarded with all these facts. But it still wasn't sinking in that she could die. Or maybe I was just trying to blank the possibility from my mind; maybe I didn't want to acknowledge just how ill Mum was.

Word had reached the press that Mum was seriously ill and I was being plagued with phone calls wanting a comment from me. It did strike me that if Vicky was alive and read a story stating her mum was ill, then surely that would prompt her to get in touch. But I didn't need any distractions so I put them off. My priority was to get Mum well again.

The doctor had warned me that after a week on a ventilator Mum could suffer further complications, even brain damage. So it was with a degree of trepidation that I turned up for visiting that day. I couldn't believe my eyes when I walked into the room. She was sitting up in bed and she was no longer attached to the machine that had been helping her breathe. She smiled as she saw me approach her bed.

This was unreal. Just 24 hours earlier Mum had looked as if she was at death's door. Now she was sitting up as if she was wondering what all the fuss was about. I sat beside her bed and started to talk. She had no recollection of me visiting her before today and couldn't remember anything of the previous week.

Then she said something that literally made the hairs on the back of my neck stand up. She said she didn't have much time left and glanced at the clock hanging on the wall. She asked me to call my uncle Ian – her brother – and ask him to come and visit her as quickly as possible. Then Mum turned to me and said: 'When you find Vicky, put her to rest beside me.'

I stared at her. What was she talking about? She was out of her coma. She was going to get better. But she kept asking for Ian, and I asked Les to call him straight away; to tell him Mum was awake and to come to the hospital. Ian arrived within 20 minutes, and when he walked in he looked as stunned as I had to see Mum sitting up and talking. Les and I left them alone.

When he emerged from Mum's room ten minutes later I walked down the hospital corridor with him. He said that Mum had told him that she hoped Vicky would be found before she died and that if she wasn't my dad would try to take control of everything. She also reiterated that when Vicky was found she wanted her buried beside her.

'But Mum's getting better. She isn't going to die.'

Ian just looked at me and smiled.

The next day Mum was hooked up to a host of machines again – there seemed to be even more this time. As soon as I entered the room a doctor told me he wanted to speak to me privately in the family room. He looked serious, and immediately my stomach began churning. In a calm voice he told me that Mum had had a relapse and that the outlook wasn't good. Then he looked me straight in the eye and said there was no hope and perhaps I should consider switching her life-support machine off so she could slip away peacefully.

I just sat there staring at him. Was this for real? How could I switch her machine off? To end her life just like that? He had just told me Mum was going to die. But she was my mum. She couldn't die. I needed her. The twins needed her. And I couldn't switch her off just like that.

I asked the doctor why he was putting the burden on me. He apologised and promised to re-evaluate the situation in 24 hours.

I walked back into Mum's room, sat down and spoke to her.

'If you can hear me, Mum, please get better. You have to get better,' I whispered into her ear. 'Please, please,

Mum. I love you. Don't leave me. I need you to help me find Vicky.' She looked peaceful, as if all the troubles she had had to face in the last few years had suddenly left her.

The next day, just after 9 a.m., my phone rang. It was one of the nurses at the hospital: 'It's time. Come to the hospital as soon as you can.'

My heart was racing as Les and I drove to Falkirk. Surely this can't be true. This can't be happening now. When I walked into Mum's room I immediately noticed she wasn't hooked up to any machines and her room was eerie and absolutely quiet. She lay motionless on the bed.

The nurse asked if I would like to wash Mum and comb her hair. I said I would and I asked Les to go and phone my Uncle Ian to tell him to come to the hospital. He had been gone less than a minute when the nurse suddenly said: 'She's leaving us.' I panicked and ran into the corridor to try and find Les. I shouted his name at the top of my voice, but he was nowhere to be seen.

I ran back into the room, tears streaming down my face. I leaned over Mum's bed and cradled her head as she gave one last shallow breath. She was gone. My beautiful, precious mother was dead.

She was only 41 years old.

I fell to the floor sobbing. She was still in the same room as me, but already I missed her desperately.

Chapter Eight

THE DAYS LEADING up to Mum's funeral were a blur. Even looking back now there is little I can remember in any kind of detail. I had lost the one person who was dearest to me and the hurt I was feeling was indescribable.

Now I had to turn my attention not only to the funeral, though, but, more importantly, to the other two people in my life now who needed me most – the twins.

Thankfully, my auntie Helen said she would take care of the arrangements for the funeral. Mum was to be buried alongside my gran at Muiravonside Cemetery in the grounds of the church where Mum and Dad married. We had agreed on a small ceremony at Cuthills Funeral Parlour in Bo'ness, and on the day it was jam-packed. People were lining the streets as I arrived in the funeral car. So many faces, so many people wanting to pay their last respects to a woman who had spent the last two years of her life struggling to cope with the trauma of losing a child, and who had died before she was able to find out the truth behind why Vicky disappeared.

Her death certificate may have listed the medical reasons why Mum died so young, but I know better than anyone the emotional toll Vicky's disappearance took on her. After that she was never the same strong and formidable woman she had been.

Mum changed for ever on the night Vicky disappeared. She tried so hard to move on, but the stress of dealing with everything surrounding Vicky's case became a sort of psychological cancer that slowly killed her. It may sound clichéd to say Mum died of a broken heart, but I truly believe she did.

I barely remember Mum's funeral service. I tried to concentrate on remembering her as she was and not on the woman I saw lying on a hospital bed surrounded by wires and tubes. I fought against my grief and remembered the good times.

At the cemetery a cord was placed in my hand. Normally there are six cords placed around the coffin to allow it to be lowered into the ground and they are reserved for close members of the family or friends. I was given cord number one, the position for the next of kin or head of the family. And that's what I was now, the head of my little family. I looked across Mum's open grave and saw Lee standing there. Just eight years old and he was being handed cord number two so that he could help lower his own mother into the ground.

Before the funeral I had taken the twins aside and carefully explained to them what a funeral service was, and afterwards I gave them the choice of whether or not they wanted to go. Lindsay didn't want to, and I didn't argue. I just told her that was fine. Lee wanted to be there. So here he was standing opposite me, a little boy looking lost and bewildered. I just wanted to reach over and hug him and make it all better. But I couldn't.

I heard some of the mourners gasp as Lee took hold of the cord. Maybe they thought someone so young shouldn't be attending their own mother's funeral, but it was Lee's choice, and one he does not regret to this day.

As I lowered Mum into the ground, I felt alone. She was my mother, but we were really friends. Her death had come upon me so quickly, and I was lost without her. I mouthed my goodbye and blew her a kiss before stepping back from the graveside.

As I did so I glanced up and saw the unmistakable figure of my dad lurking in the background. I walked past and pretended I hadn't seen him. He was the last person I wanted to speak to on a day like this. He didn't help my mum after Vicky disappeared. Why should I speak to him now?

The days that followed Mum's funeral were ghastly. Her house seemed to be a procession of people coming and going, making sure I was all right, and that the twins were fine. We were living in a bit of a bubble, and it was only towards the end of that week that I had time to myself to sit down and think properly about the consequences of Mum's death.

Children are very resilient, and the twins had coped well considering the circumstances. But I knew the next decision I had to take would impact on them for the rest of their lives. Mum's words from all those years ago when I was just 14 kept on coming back to me. 'If anything happens to me, you must take care of the twins.' She had said this to me with such conviction that I had never forgotten it.

At the time I had truly believed that this situation would never occur and that Mum would live to a ripe old age and the twins would grow up to live their own lives with Mum there as their support. I never once thought that at the age of 22 I would have to fulfil the promise I'd made to Mum eight years earlier.

Now here I was faced with the daunting reality. Mum was gone; Vicky was missing; Dad had shown no interest in the twins after he walked out. I was the only one left.

Would Dad step forward and offer to take the twins in? I wasn't convinced.

There was no doubt in my mind what I had to do. I

would 'adopt' the twins and would raise them as my own. I would carry out my promise to Mum.

I probably didn't fully appreciate the enormity of the decision. I was barely into my twenties and engaged. I had a lot of opportunities in front of me. But I knew that, despite the pressures bringing up two children would bring, I really wanted to do this. I needed to do this for Mum. I had to keep this family together so that when Vicky came home she had somewhere safe and secure to come to.

The only small doubt in my mind was Les. How would he react to this? He never imagined that when he asked me to marry him he was getting a ready-made family as a job lot. I would have to square it with him, but I'd already made up my mind that no matter what his reaction was, I was going to adopt Lee and Lindsay.

I sat down with Les and told him my plans. I gave him the opportunity to walk away. I told him I would understand and think no less of him if he did. To my eternal relief he said he had no doubt in *his* mind. He wanted me and he wanted my family.

Now I had to speak to Dad – the moment I was dreading. I went to his house and sat down with him, and in the most civil way I could I asked him if he had thought about the twins' future. He actually offered to let Lee and Lindsay live with him and Christine. When I said I wanted them to live with me he didn't object but said the offer was there and if I decided that they should live with him, I should just call him.

I remember thinking that Mum would be pleased that he had no objection to the twins living with me. That is what she would have wanted.

In the end I didn't see the need to go through the long, drawn-out formal legal process of having to adopt the twins to keep them with me. I was their big sister, and as long as nobody objected and the social work department were satisfied I was a fit and responsible person, then everyone was happy with the arrangement.

It was all set. I was going to be their new 'mum'.

Looking back, I can't remember sitting the twins down and explaining my decision to them. It just sort of happened. It felt natural to me that I should take care of them.

In hindsight it was one of the hardest – and easiest – decisions of my life. Over the years the twins have expressed their gratitude many times for what I did for them, but I feel fully repaid because of the unconditional love they have shown me.

I couldn't face the prospect of us all moving into Mum's house. It was hard enough when I had to go there to take her personal belongings away. There were so many bad memories there now that we all needed a fresh start.

So the four of us crammed into Les's one-bedroom flat. We put the twins' bunk beds up in the corner of the living room. It was a real squeeze, but we simply made do. I was so proud of Les; his life was turned upside down overnight and he never complained.

The Social Services were on hand to help out too. We didn't want to disrupt the twins' lives any more than we had to. Taking them out of their family home and away from their friends must have been terrible for them and they were being so brave. So we decided to let them stay on at school until we were allocated a larger local authority house. Social Services organised a lovely woman to come and collect the kids and take them to and from school. It was a godsend.

I decided too, that I should get a day job while the kids where at school. We had mouths to feed. Les tried to get a full-time job too, but in the meantime we ran karaoke sessions at the pub at the weekend to keep us afloat.

A friend of a friend was a secretary for a local garage and she said they were looking for office staff. I sailed through the interview and landed a part-time job at their truck depot just outside Falkirk. It was just the boost we needed. The only thing that was holding us back now was where we lived. We simply couldn't afford to buy anything bigger. Luckily we were able to call on Les's Mum and Dad Tommy and Catherine who lived around the corner. They were a great support to us and we arranged to store some of Mum's furniture in their garage.

Over the next few weeks I was up to my eyes trying to get us a council house, work at my new job and make sure the twins were happy. All the while I was ignoring a dull pain in my stomach. Eventually, after much nagging from Les I went to see the doctor. He suggested further tests in hospital and I was diagnosed with a stomach ulcer, probably, according to the specialist, brought on by the stress of the last two years.

We were still very shaken up as a family, and my sickness showed me just how vulnerable Lee and Lindsay felt. The twins didn't like the fact that I was ill and needed to go to the hospital. They associated the hospital with death, and immediately asked me if, like Mum, I was going to die. They thought I was going to leave them, too, like Vicky had. I sat them both down and told them that I would always be there for them, not just now, but for ever.

Since Vicky had disappeared, and after Mum died, Lindsay thought our family was cursed; she even said so on a number of occasions. The twins both remember Vicky and how she used to spend hours playing with them, but they were very young, and had no real concept of where she had gone or what might have happened to her.

Telling them about Vicky has been a gradual process over the years and, as they grew older, they came to accept that it was very unlikely they would ever see her again. They had it drummed into them, firstly by Mum and then by me, about 'bad men' and 'strange cars'. Mum and I were both convinced Vicky had been abducted and I suppose we were consequently over-protective of the twins. They grew up with their sister missing and, in a strange way, got used to it at an early age. They have both said many times that they miss her, but, tragically, I feel they never really got to know her properly.

I suppose we must have been moved to the top of the housing list because of our circumstances, and a few weeks after I left hospital, we were allocated a council house in Bainsford, an area of Falkirk. It was a three-bedroom semi-detached just around the corner from Tommy and Catherine's house. In fact you could see their spare bedroom window from our living room. The house seemed huge compared to the tiny flat we were used to, and best of all, the garden was enormous – plenty of room for the twins to run around and play. When I walked through the front door, it immediately felt like home, and I couldn't help thinking that wherever Mum was she was happy for us. We were a family again, in a proper family home.

We were all settled in no time. I got the twins into the local primary school and within days they had already made new friends.

Les had been applying for loads of jobs, but nothing came of his efforts. He was getting more and more into a domestic routine with the twins while I went out to work. He cooked the tea and did the necessary everyday chores. The twins didn't come home to an empty house and we didn't have to pay for childcare. The social work department said they were delighted with the arrangement, and signed us off their books. They could see that we were a settled family unit and that the twins wanted for nothing and were content.

The search for Vicky was continuing, and the police were in touch from time to time, but I could tell they were frustrated. There were no new leads and the detectives had nothing to go on. They were going over old ground. My sister's disappearance was just as baffling two years on as it was the night she went missing.

*

I didn't even know Les had entered the competition in the *Falkirk Herald* for Bride of the Year – so I was shocked to discover in the paper that Les and I were in the final six. The prize was a dream all-expenses-paid wedding worth around £7,000. The *Herald* reporter came to our house, and I recognised him immediately. He had written a number of articles about Vicky; I had also seen him at Mum's funeral. He was a kind, gentle man and he seemed genuinely concerned about my family. He confided in me that Les and I had actually won the competition and asked us to keep the result secret before the big finals night at Falkirk Town Hall.

I was stunned. At last some good news, and I think we deserved it after all we had been through. The reporter said that I should act surprised when the final result was announced and I should have been given an Oscar! Despite knowing the result, I still got a thrill out of the evening.

We had our wedding paid for now, which was a huge financial relief. The competition win took care of the cost of my wedding dress, car hire, photography, the band, the cake and all the extras. But things still had to be organised. Catherine was a fantastic help. She was simply brilliant, doing all the things Mum would have done had she still been alive.

We booked Old St Modan's Church in Falkirk with the reception in the nearby Park Hotel. I'd asked the twins to take official roles at the wedding – Lee as a page boy and Lindsay as a bridesmaid. Les had asked his friend David to be best man, and I was delighted to have Angela as my maid of honour.

Chapter Eight

Of course, at this time I thought a lot about Vicky. Angela was doing the things that Vicky would have been doing if she had been there: helping me with the arrangements, my hair and my make-up.

I would have given anything for her to have been with me in the weeks running up to the wedding. I know she would have been trying to boss me around, and attempting to give me advice on what to wear and how to do my hair. I would have ignored all her suggestions, just out of sisterly obstinacy, but, oh, how I would have given anything just to hear her voice.

Everything was set for a wonderful day. Even my granny Hamilton – my dad's mum – planned to fly in from South Africa. The only two people I really wanted to be there, however, were Mum and Vicky. Oh, how I missed them, and the gap in my life was simply magnified when I was arranging what should have been the happiest day of my life. They both should have been there.

I also had a decision to make about whether my father should be at the wedding. I had vowed some years before that I would never allow him to walk me down the aisle on my wedding day, and at the time I had meant it. However, I had grown up a lot over the years and felt it was important that nothing should mar the day Les and I had planned. So I relented and asked Dad if he would be there for me. He was delighted and said he would be honoured.

It was yet another olive branch to him. I was 22, and I had changed. Maybe Dad had too. Maybe his days of being an absent father were over. I hoped that the wedding would help us build a better relationship.

There was one thing I was sure of with regard to our wedding, however. There was absolutely no way that I was inviting Christine. When I told Dad this he was shocked and couldn't understand why. I told him I didn't think it was appropriate that she should attend. I said if Mum had been alive Christine wouldn't have been invited, and I felt that I would be betraying her by inviting Christine to the wedding. So the decision was made.

On 12 August 1993, I walked down the aisle with my father holding my arm and married Les. In spite of the fact that it was tinged with sadness, with two such important people missing, it was a fantastic day – one of the happiest of my life.

There was the usual press interest as there always was when something significant happened. But I took the view that any publicity about the wedding was also going to mention Vicky's case, and after so long without any real developments, it was worth the extra hassle.

I think the newspapers thought that, if Vicky had run away, she would turn up again on this day of all days. I admit that when I arrived at the church I found myself looking around for her; I was gazing into the countryside, hoping and praying that she would just walk around the corner and say: 'Hey, Sis. I'm here.' I knew it was stupid, but I was looking for a miracle. I knew in my heart it wouldn't happen.

Dad didn't stay long at the reception, and I was sad to see him leave so early, but I understood why he did. At least for once he had done the right thing. He'd performed his duties. I wouldn't say I was proud of him for being there that day, but I'm glad he turned up.

The day after the wedding I drove up to Mum's grave at Muiravonside and laid my bouquet beside her headstone. I told her about the wedding and that I was missing her. I also told her that, for the first time for a while, I was happy.

*

Les and I went to Torquay for our honeymoon. It was the first time we had been away from the twins since Mum died. They were being looked after by Tommy and Catherine, and I phoned them every night. We arrived home to a mass of presents and cards; we were overwhelmed by the generosity of friends and family. But one card stood out from the bundle that I read on our first day back. It was unusual because it was addressed to the church where we got married. Staff at the church had re-addressed it and sent it on to us. I opened the envelope and took out the card. The message read: 'Congratulations

on your wedding day from Wilma and your sister Vicky.'
I got such a fright I immediately dropped the card on the
table. 'Les. Call the police straight away.'

At the back of my mind I was sure that the card was a
hoax, but it was still a terrible feeling seeing Vicky's name
there. 'It must be a crank,' I thought. And yet again I
wondered what kind of sick person would do such a thing.

CID came round straight away and took the card away
for fingerprinting. They assured me it would most likely
be a hoax, but they were obviously determined to find out
who was behind it. It didn't take them long. A woman
with psychological problems was charged and taken to
court. I decided I wanted to see her face to face. I don't
know why – I suppose to try and understand why she
would do such a thing. But she never turned up to the
hearing. She was eventually jailed, and I was happy that
the police and the courts took the whole matter seriously.

Despite this difficult start, Les and I settled down to
married life. Tommy and Catherine had become adoptive
grandparents for the twins and they were a fantastic help.
The twins regularly spent the weekend over at their house
to allow Les and me to work. In addition to my day job at
the garage, we had our own karaoke business now and we
were kept busy.

The search for Vicky, however, was going nowhere,
and it was extremely depressing. I could go for weeks

without hearing from the CID, and I had to continuously try and think of ways to keep her case in the spotlight. Without Mum around, it was down to me to keep the pressure on and liaise with the police. The newspapers didn't seem too interested in Dad since his outburst about the police, so I was the one they called. The newspapers could be fickle and took the view that if there were no real developments there wasn't a story. So I often agreed to magazine interviews to keep Vicky's name in the public domain. It was difficult trying to think of new angles and I became more interested in the general subject of missing people in the UK. I felt it was important to raise awareness of the issue and it was a vehicle I could use to remind people of the circumstances of Vicky's disappearance.

During the next couple of years I appeared in countless magazines. But I also took part in a number of national TV shows. I met some interesting people, especially when I appeared on the chat shows like *Kilroy* and *Esther*, but all of the shows were nerve-racking. With every one I had the same routine: I pictured Vicky and Mum in my mind's eye before going in front of the cameras. It gave me strength to get through the ordeal and I grew more and more confident in TV studios the more I appeared.

And it was all a means to an end. An attempt to keep Vicky's name in lights in the hope that just one viewer might remember something or find it within themselves to come forward.

*

My relationship with my father around this time was, as ever, strained. I think I was somehow always looking for him to say he was proud of me. I only remember him telling me once that he loved me.

Over the years I have tried very hard to fit in with his new family, but there was always a barrier there, and I was never able to breach it. After Nicole was born in 1984, Dad and Christine had two more children – Kirsty in 1986 and young Michael in 1989. Dad has always kept his 'new' family separate, and there has been little crossover through the years – that is the way he seemed to want it.

I've never held any grudge against any of Dad's children. After all, the break-up of my family had nothing to do with them. Obviously, they have a loyalty to their father, and I'm sure they don't appreciate my views on him.

Dad would never argue against Christine. Every single time there were cross words said between me and Christine, he would say nothing. Every single time Dad let me down, and I just picked up the pieces and moved on.

My regular disagreements with my dad were really the only trauma I had to deal with now. Things had settled down. The twins seemed very contented and Les and I were sublimely happy. I was glad that finally, after the emotional turmoil of the previous few years with Vicky's disappearance and Mum's death, that perhaps we would enjoy a period of stability. I should have known better.

*

It was four years since Vicky had disappeared and we'd never managed to get away on holiday, mostly for financial reasons. I was delighted when Tommy and Catherine said they were going for a break to Blackpool and asked me if it was okay to take the twins along.

Tommy had had some problems with his heart and the doctors had warned him to give up smoking. He and Catherine were keen to get some sea air, so they booked the trip.

The twins were ten now and I was so pleased for them as this would be their first ever holiday. Mum could never afford to take them when she was alive, and unfortunately her time ran out before she got the opportunity. When we told them, their little faces lit up with glee. They began saving up for spending money, doing any odd job they could. I told them stories all about the Blackpool funfair and it was great to see them so excited and animated.

When the big day arrived they set off skipping down the front path to the car. This wasn't just their first holiday; it was their first time away from home. I was pleased for them but scared at the same time. I so hoped nothing would go wrong.

Les and I worked our shifts at the pub that night and it was after 1 a.m. when we arrived home. We had Tommy and Catherine's pet poodle Vanity as a house guest while they were away, and when we went to bed she snuggled up on top of the covers at the foot of the bed.

We had just drifted off to sleep, when Vanity started making slight whimpering noises. Then she started barking loudly. She jumped off the bed and walked to the top of the staircase. I yelled at her to stop. Les was sound asleep. Then the phone rang downstairs and I heard the answering machine kicking in. I lay silently in bed, straining to hear. I could hear a man's voice, but I couldn't quite make out what he was saying. I jumped out of bed, heart racing, and yelled at Les to get up. There was something wrong, I just knew it. I ran downstairs and played the message. It was George, Les's brother-in-law, saying something had happened at Blackpool.

I started shaking and saying, 'Oh please, God no.' Before I knew it I was hysterical. I don't know how I knew, but I had an overwhelming feeling that Les's father had died. Sadly, I was right; Tommy had died of a heart attack in his sleep.

I suppose I was relieved that nothing had happened to

the twins, but I felt terribly sorry for Les. He had supported me with the ups and downs after Vicky's disappearance, and helped me through the tough times when Mum died. Now he had to face the death of a parent as well. It seemed that our lives were blighted by tragedy at every turn.

Les and I drove all the way to Blackpool. When we arrived Tommy's body had been taken to the mortuary. Catherine was still in the holiday chalet, sitting watching over the twins, who had slept right through all the goings-on. She looked absolutely drained. You could tell she had been crying most of the night but she had bravely sat there looking after the twins throughout while her own husband lay dead.

I went into the twins' room, and I could hear Lindsay quietly sobbing under her bed covers. She had overheard us talking and was devastated. When we told Lee he too burst into tears. Tommy was the closest thing they had to a grandfather.

The twins were so young and had been through so much in their short lives. It must have been confusing. People around them were either dying or disappearing. I felt more protective of them than ever before.

Over the next few weeks I was haunted by a paranoia that something was going to happen to the twins. I was convinced that someone was going to try and take them away; abduct them and then hurt them. They say lightning doesn't strike twice in the same place, but I couldn't take that chance. After we'd lost Vicky, I couldn't bear the thought of anything happening to Lee or Lindsay. I preached at them about strangers and about not getting into cars with anyone they didn't know. I also devised a code system. In the unlikely event that Les or I couldn't collect them from school a password would be used to let the twins know that it was safe to get a lift from someone else.

I thought back to how heartbreaking it was to lose Vicky; to have her snatched away in the blink of an eye. I felt vulnerable, so I could only imagine how fragile and insecure the twins were feeling. I would have done anything to protect my new family, and I wasn't about to let anything happen to the twins. They were all I had left.

*

The fifth anniversary of Vicky's disappearance slipped by quietly. As I always do, I marked the occasion in my own way and lit a candle for Vicky. In comparison to previous years, the newspaper interest was limited. The story had gone cold, and there was very little I could do to stimulate interest except grasp every opportunity that came along, no matter how unlikely.

I was approached by the producers of a live daytime chat show hosted by the television presenter Kirsty Young.

They wanted me to take part in their debate about psychics; Ann Anderson was scheduled to be on the show too, along with another woman called Mary. I was very nervous but Les agreed to come on the show with me. There was nothing to lose and it was a chance to get Vicky's picture on the television again.

The audience reacted badly to Ann Anderson when Kirsty Young recounted the story of her claiming she had found Vicky's earring. I barely said a word. I was determined to keep my dignity on TV. I think the producers wanted me to criticise Ann Anderson, but it was Les who did most of the talking. He knew how I felt about finding Vicky and how I was willing to hold on to anything that would help me find her.

Then events took an unexpected twist. Mary said she wasn't a psychic but used a Ouija board to contact the dead, and she had something important to say to me. The audience fell hushed as she told me she had received a message from Vicky who was on the 'other side'. She took out a piece of paper and began reading from notes she said she had taken during her 'conversation' with Vicky.

I felt the camera zoom in on me, trying to catch my reaction to her words. She said that Vicky wanted to get a message to her family to tell us that she got in a car with a man the night she disappeared. I couldn't hear any more. I just heard the word car and my mind went blank. Mary kept on talking, but I wasn't taking it in. Here I was again, listening to the words of a woman I'd never met before, giving me messages supposedly from beyond the grave.

I suppose when you are desperate to find something out you will grab at any possible source, so it was with some trepidation that I found myself making an arrangement with Mary to visit her at her home after the show.

She lived in Cumbernauld, near Glasgow, and when she showed me into her kitchen I was surprised to find she had already set up her Ouija board on the table. I sat down next to her, and Les and her husband took the other two chairs. She began to 'talk' to Vicky. She must have tried about ten times before eventually she gave up, saying that the spirit was too weak to talk. That was it for me. I had had enough of these women and their so-called ability to talk to the 'other side'. Who did they think they were? Coming into people's lives concocting tales. Playing with people's vulnerability and feeding off their weaknesses. I had had it. All they seemed to me to be were eccentric people, with nothing better to do with their time. From now on, I wanted nothing more to do with them.

It is amazing, however, how they have an ability to draw you in. I mentioned Mary to Dad, and goodness knows why, but he decided to meet her too. It is funny now, but he was so convinced about what she was telling him that he went with her to an area in Stirling where he began digging in among some bushes and trees looking for Vicky's remains.

My dad nearly collapsed when he unearthed a huge black plastic bag with something inside it – until it turned out to be a bag full of old junk. The whole experience scared Dad a bit, however, and he also vowed never to have anything to do with psychics again.

*

Two years after our wedding, Les and I began trying for a baby and, after just a few months, I found out I was pregnant. I was full of joy. At last we had something good to look forward too. We gently broke the news to the twins, and they were thrilled.

I called Dad at work to tell him the news. He sounded delighted about becoming a grandfather, and joked about being too young. Little Emma-Jane was born eight days late, on 4 December 1996. Dad was one of the first to the hospital. He grinned from ear to ear when he held her. She was perfect and beautiful. She was all I ever hoped she would be. She brought a ray of sunshine back, not only into my life but the twins' and Catherine's lives too.

After my six months' maternity leave, I returned to work full-time at the garage. I left Les and Catherine to look after the kids. I hated going to work, even more so because I was separated from my baby daughter, but I knew she was in safe hands. I thought about her all day long, wondering what she would be doing, until I couldn't stand it any more. I told Les that I would look for part-time work, and that he could find a job that could work with or around the hours that we needed childcare.

I felt things had started looking up for us. Emma-Jane was coming on great and had bonded with the twins. Family life was hard work but rewarding too.

The next eighteen months were harmonious as far as my home life was concerned, but during that spell there were absolutely no developments in the hunt for Vicky. I spoke to the police every few weeks, but always the answer was the same: nothing happening.

Sadly, during the entire time that Vicky was missing there were long periods – sometimes years – when there were no new leads. I know the police were working tire-lessly, but they had nothing new to go on. It was heartbreaking, and there was very little I could do and I appreciated it was frustrating for the police too.

However, I had put one landmark date in my diary. The seventh anniversary of Vicky's disappearance was fast approaching. In Scotland if someone is missing for that length of time, they can officially be declared dead. If she was 'legally' dead it would mean the end to her case. It would be closed, and we would never find out what happened to her. I knew I didn't want that to happen, but

I also realised I needed to get Dad on board as he was officially her next of kin.

I was very nervous about broaching this subject with Dad. I couldn't think of any reason why he would want Vicky declared dead, but with Dad you just never know. I went to see him and explained the situation. To my relief he said he agreed with me and didn't want to take a decision that would effectively bring her life to a close. I was so pleased, and I hoped that one day we would find out what really happened to Vicky.

On the anniversary I did a few more magazine and newspaper interviews, but I was starting to think it was all in vain. I was certain that someone out there knew of Vicky's whereabouts, and I had a feeling that we might never find him until he abducted some other girl. I truly believed that one day Vicky's abductor would slip up. Appeals in the press for information weren't coming to anything, but I was determined to keep on telling Vicky's story even though I had to work harder than ever to keep her memory and case alive. We hardly ever heard from the police. Vicky's case was cold. Since her purse was found, there had been no other leads into her disappearance.

I found a part-time job working in the cash office for a large record shop chain in Falkirk. It fitted in with my busy life and gave me the opportunity to provide for my family and spend quality time with them too. The twins were growing up fast, especially Lindsay. She was always testing the boundaries with Les and me. She eventually got in with a bad crowd at school and her previously good grades were turning bad. I felt she was slowly going off the rails.

And gradually Lindsay started to go downhill emotionally. She disappeared within herself and started taking her frustrations out in a destructive way. She cut Christine and Dad out of her life. She refused to visit them and simply sat in the car if I was at Dad's house.

Poor Lindsay got on to a rocky road, and I worried so much about her. Eventually we ended up arranging counselling sessions to try and address her problems. We decided to take her out of her high school, and move her to another one, in the hope that she would eventually settle down. It was a difficult decision but when we saw the results in her grades, we had realised we made the right move in getting her away from the bad crowd she was hanging around with.

We were trying our best to raise the twins, but there were unbelievable stresses and strains in dealing with two young teenagers at the same time. The fact I was relatively young too meant I had an understanding of what they were going through, but that didn't make it any easier. It is safe to say we had our ups and downs with both of them, but every time there was a problem I would just grit my teeth, think of Mum and get on with it. Lindsay joked that she was only staying with us until she was 16, then she would flee the nest and get her own flat. I wasn't against the idea – after all, I left home young.

But Lindsay reminded me so much of Vicky. She had that strong will and typical teenage obstinacy that Vicky had before she disappeared. Vicky went through a spell where you couldn't give her advice, and if you tried to she would just ignore it anyway. Lindsay was exactly the same. Their moods were so alike it was spooky. I realised if I was going to steer Lindsay away from the direction she was going in, I would need all my resolve.

Then, just after the twins' 16th birthday, Lindsay applied for and was offered a flat by the local council. I must admit I was very concerned about her moving out, but I knew that if I tried to argue with her it would end up in a huge row. She was very determined. I suppose she reminded me of myself when I was planning to set up home in Livingston and had to break the news to Mum. Mum and I had an almighty argument then, and I didn't want to have the same situation with Lindsay. I bit my tongue and made out I was happy for her, but all the time I was eaten up inside with worry. I consoled myself with the fact that the flat was just ten minutes' walk from our house, so it meant we were on hand if she needed anything. As soon as she got the keys, we all helped out with the decorating and with filling it with furniture.

Lindsay wasn't entitled to much financial help from the government and she was finding it hard to survive. She had a part-time job already working in a shoe shop at the weekends but she was only in the flat a few months when she had to leave her fifth year at school and find a job to help her pay the rent. She was offered a full-time position and accepted. She put her education to one side but vowed to take it up again once she had found her feet.

Dad had got Lee his first real job working at the local bus factory valeting the buses, and a few months later Lee moved into Lindsay's spare room. I felt proud of them both. They were growing up very quickly and Lindsay in particular had turned a corner. She was determined to lead her own life.

Frankly I had struggled on many occasions to cope with 'motherhood' after it was unexpectedly thrust upon me. But I loved the twins and I would have done anything for them.

Their childhood had been destroyed by Vicky's disappearance and being robbed of their mother. I had been determined not to let Mum down and to fulfil the promise I had made to her. The twins didn't need me so much now and they were making their own way in the world. We – and they in particular – had travelled a shaky road and yet somehow managed to pull through it all.

Chapter Nine

TIME WAS MOVING swiftly on. So swiftly that it was soon the tenth anniversary of Vicky going missing. A lot had happened in that time. Mum had died and I had become the twins' surrogate mother. Les and I were married, and we had a daughter, Emma-Jane. But we still hadn't found Vicky. I was living my life, but underneath everything lay an awful emptiness. I was growing older, while Vicky remained that 15-year-old girl I had last seen boarding a bus.

I often wondered, 'What if?' What would Vicky have been like as an aunt? Would she have fulfilled her dream of becoming a vet? If Mum had got to meet her first grand-child, would she have spoiled her rotten, like grans often do? I missed them so much. It was hard to accept that a decade had passed since I waved Vicky off that night.

The police were now openly accepting that this was a murder hunt, though there were still precious few clues, and nobody in the family or those who knew Vicky thought otherwise. Someone must have abducted her that night and killed her. It was the only possible explanation for an ordinary schoolgirl to simply disappear. I accepted Vicky was dead, but we had no grave to visit; nowhere we could lay flowers and remember her.

I knew the tenth anniversary would be the trigger for renewed police and press activity, and I mentally braced myself for the onslaught. For many reasons the big day was a bit of a damp squib. The police had nothing new to go on, but were determined to get Vicky's name in the newspapers and on the TV again. I supported them in all their suggestions, which included setting up a temporary police 'station' in Bathgate near where Vicky was last seen, in the hope that someone might come forward.

The police also produced a computer-generated image of what Vicky might have looked like aged 25. I have to confess I laughed out loud when they showed me the picture. It looked to me as though they had simply stuck Mum's hairstyle onto Vicky's face. I thought it was point-less, but I couldn't tell the police that. After all, they were willing to try anything to get the vital breakthrough they had worked so hard for and anything that might help was worth it.

The picture produced a feeding frenzy for the press. At last they had something concrete to report. The police held a press conference at which they unveiled the 'image' of Vicky, and the next day every single national newspaper carried the picture alongside articles about the tenth anniversary. So, the police achieved their goal, and for that I was grateful.

For my part, I agreed to carry out a number of press interviews outlining my thoughts ten years on. The newspapers are always keen to speak to me rather than Dad, as I was the last member of the family to see Vicky alive. But it was a bit like going over the same ground as I had done so many times over the years.

By now I had become impervious to the whole media circus. And, sadly, I had begun to believe that after all this time it wasn't going to do any good. I accepted for the first time that there was a better than average chance that the mystery of what happened to my little sister might never be solved.

As far as I am aware, the new image and all the interviews served little purpose, and the police received scant feedback for their efforts. It was demoralising for the hard-working officers and for the family. It was becoming harder and harder to cope with the disappointments.

I was also aware, and had been for some time, that the strain of the previous few years was taking its toll on my marriage. It wasn't a sudden thing, but a gradual rotting away of something that once had been so good. I wasn't happy, and more and more I began to see Les as a father figure instead of the man I had fallen in love with.

It was a mixture of factors that finally ended it in 2001. I suppose part of it was me finally growing up. I'd been married for seven years, brought up two children and was now bringing up a third, and I seemed to have less and less in common with my husband. I tried to fight the feelings, but it was no use. I had to be true to myself and finish it.

It was hard to leave the family home, but I felt I had no choice, I needed to find myself again. Having been a surrogate mother to the twins, working all hours and being Vicky's spokesperson, I'd lost my own identity in the mayhem.

I didn't want to take Emma-Jane away from her father. Given our own childhood, I'm a strong believer that children need both parents' influence on their upbringing. I might have not loved Les any more but he was still a good dad. So Les and I agreed to have joint custody of Emma-Jane.

At first she spent one week at a flat I'd rented in nearby New Carron Village, and the next at her dad's. Emma-Jane soon adjusted to her new routine, and it wasn't long before we extended it to two weeks at each place. That way it gave us each more time to do more things with her.

It was around this time that I started to feel ill. I felt tired all the time and I simply got fed up with life. I felt down in the dumps from the moment I opened my eyes until I went to bed. I would burst into tears for no apparent reason. It is not something that happened suddenly, but a feeling that crept up on me. At one particularly low point I even thought about the ways I could harm myself. Luckily I never tried to, but it was an indication of how far I'd sunk.

I went to see my doctor and he concluded I was suffering from depression. He prescribed antidepressants. He said my condition was brought about by a number of factors, but was mostly a culmination of the stress and the anxiety I had had to face over the past decade. I also believed my tempestuous relationship with my father was one of the underlying factors in my condition. He is the man I so wanted to be loved by, yet I felt he wasn't there for me when I needed him.

I suffered terrible mood swings. I lost my confidence. This was a dark and gloomy time, and I'm not sure how I came out the other side, but gradually, after a few months, my mood lifted and I began to see a way forward.

Possibly it was the thought of what I would do to the twins that stopped me from suicide or self-harming. I still to this day suffer from bouts of depression, but medication and the support of my family helps me through the bad spells. It is now sadly a problem which will probably always be with me. It lies dormant for so long, then something triggers it again and I go into a downward spiral.

I had applied for and managed to get a brilliant job in retail banking with one of the biggest banks in Scotland. It was a fantastic break for me and it was the kind of job I never believed I would have. The man who helped rebuild my confidence and made me believe in myself to get the job was someone from my past.

I'd worked with Brian two years earlier at the Virgin record store in Falkirk, but he'd moved to another store shortly after I started work. By coincidence we met again at a function, and immediately got chatting about old times. We realised we wanted to spend more time together, and friendship soon blossomed into romance.

I fell madly in love. Brian was just the tonic I needed. He helped me get my life sorted out, and recognised my problems. He literally lifted me out of my depression and gave me new strength. I give him full credit for sorting my head out and making me believe I could get that job.

We had a great deal in common. Brian lived in Bathgate when Vicky went missing. He also used to drink in the pub that I worked in, although I had never seen him there. He is the same age as me, and I love reminiscing with him about growing up in the eighties. Brian is a very bright, articulate person. I feel at ease in his company and with him I feel safe and secure. Where I can be an extrovert,

Brian is an introvert. But we still like the same things, and, most importantly, we make each other laugh.

Like most people in Bathgate, Brian almost 'lived' the Vicky Hamilton inquiry. It was impossible to be in the town and not be aware of the police activity, especially in the early weeks. He also recalls seeing the 'iconic' police poster of Vicky, bearing her picture, the one in her in her school uniform, displayed on lampposts and shop windows.

He remembers clearly the police searches in the area, and the fact they were stopping motorists almost on a daily basis to ask them questions about Vicky.

I suppose it was strange that I should fall for someone from Bathgate, the town which became synonymous with my sister's disappearance, but in a strange way it gave us an extra bond; a connection. Living in Bathgate, Brian appreciated more than most the enormity of the search for Vicky and the scale of the police inquiry.

Our relationship was going so well I took the big step of introducing him to Emma-Jane. They got on great but I always stressed to Emma-Jane that Brian wasn't going to take the place of her father. I soon introduced Brian to the rest of my family, including Dad. Their first meeting went as well as could be expected, but I could tell that Brian wasn't too keen. They are just very different people.

With Brian I felt so happy again, and I really believed we had a future together. I loved him so much.

Things were going from strength to strength in our relationship, and we decided to buy a house together in Falkirk. Emma-Jane would have a back garden to play in, and there was a child's play park right outside our front door. With no noisy neighbours upstairs and situated in a new, quiet development within walking distance to the town centre, it was perfect. It also meant that Emma-Jane wasn't far away from her school or her dad.

In spring 2003 – 12 years after Vicky disappeared – Brian's mum, Liz, called to say she was holding a 'spooky' evening at her house and asked me if I would like to come along. At first I was against the idea because of my previous encounters with the so-called spirit world, but even though I was a bit of a sceptic, I decided to go.

Liz lived in Bathgate where I was quite well known, so I decided to go in disguise. If this psychic woman was going to tell me anything I didn't want to make it easy for her by revealing I was Vicky's sister. I pulled my hair up under a black cap and I wore glasses.

When she arrived she introduced herself as Linda, and I could tell by her demeanour that she didn't recognise me. I led Linda through to the conservatory, where it was dim and quiet.

Chapter Nine

Liz had lit a few candles and strategically placed them around the room. She sat down at the table and I sat in the seat opposite. She took out some cards and placed them on top of the table. She started to ask me a question, then stopped and looked over my shoulder.

She said: 'There is a young woman here, possibly connected to you. She has her head bowed down but she has shoulder-length dark hair.'

I let her go on. 'You have a special bond with this young woman. A car pulls up, and she recognises the man. He gave her a lift.'

I couldn't believe what she was saying to me, but I was determined not to give her any clues. I was still sceptical, but obviously I was fascinated by what she was saying. I shook my head and said: 'I don't know who or what you are talking about.'

Then she said: 'You have offended the spirit.' The hairs stood up on the back of my neck, and I could feel my heart rate increase. I was being spooked. I let her continue.

'He drove through Bathgate and she is drinking from a can she is holding. He then drove through Torphicen [a village near Bathgate].' Again I insisted that it didn't make any sense to me. I was determined I wouldn't give her any clues. She went on: 'After about 15 minutes, the girl is feeling drowsy.'

Linda then demonstrated the action of being relaxed

and slumped while pretending to shake an imaginary can, while looking inside it. This is unbelievable, I thought.

'He drives over the Avon Gorge [a small bridge linking Torphicen to the village of Maddiston] and turns off the road. He is driving up a dirt track road for about one to two miles, before he comes to an old derelict farm and stops the car.'

Linda then stopped talking as she struggled to find the next words to say. She looked me in the eye and said: 'Are you sure you don't know who I'm talking about?'

'Maybe.'

Linda then said that the spirit was urging her to tell me a lot of things. Then, suddenly, she asked: 'Is it Vicky?' I nodded slowly. I watched the colour drain from her face. 'Oh my God,' she exclaimed.

'Can you tell me where Vicky is?' I stammered, barely able to form the words.

'I will do my best,' she said.

She then proceeded to tell me what the spirit had told her. She said the man who was driving the car killed Vicky. He drugged her, then drove to an old farm in a nearly village and killed her, perhaps accidentally. He left her body for over two days, then went back and took her from a shallow grave, put her back into his car and drove a few hundred yards away, up a small hill. He stopped at another derelict farmhouse that was being renovated. He took the cover off a manhole and put Vicky's body down it.

Linda also claimed that the man had a good knowledge of the area with a strong connection with Edinburgh. He wore a denim jacket and jeans, was tall, and was aged about 27.

She said the man would eventually be caught, but I wouldn't find Vicky's body for another seven years. My heart sank at the thought. How could I wait another seven years before finding her?

But Linda insisted she would be found and that waiting seven years was nothing compared to the prospect of never finding her at all. She said the police would have to do their homework to catch this man and that he had already been in trouble with the law. She said he would be caught first and then police would later find Vicky's body.

I shivered, but was fascinated by what she had told me. I tried hard to give myself a reality check; after all I'd had bad experiences with psychics before. But she was so convincing. Maybe there was something in what she was saying.

There was no way on earth she recognised me, so to pull Vicky's name out of thin air was quite remarkable. Could she really hold the key to finding my sister?

I was well over my time limit and so Linda gave me her number and told me to call her in a few days. As I drove home that night I had second thoughts about phoning Linda. Did I really want to go down that road again, of building up my hopes to have them shattered? Could I handle it emotionally? Was I ready for something like this? My heart was saying yes, but my head was saying no. I wanted to find Vicky more than anything, but could I risk being disappointed again?

It took me weeks to pluck up the courage to call Linda. I wanted to be able to ignore what she had told me, but I simply couldn't. Curiosity got the better of me. I called her and arranged to meet her at her home. I asked if I could record the meeting and she agreed.

At the meeting she went over the same information that she had told me months before, but in more detail. Linda described the area where she thought Vicky would be. She talked about Vicky being near water, a river maybe? It was dark so there was no point in searching that night, but she agreed to meet me in the area she believed Vicky was buried.

The next day I met Linda and we drove the route she believed Vicky took that night. She showed me area where she thought Vicky might be. It was a large wooded area that had a beautiful reservoir next to it. It was only a mile off the main road but it was secluded and quiet with three farms surrounding it.

She took me to the spot where she said that Vicky lay

for two days. Then suddenly Linda said that she was exhausted and 'burnt out' and that she wanted to carry on with the search another time. She was going on holiday later that week and said she would call me when she returned. I was desperate to continue, but she wouldn't.

I thought about telling Dad, but I didn't want to get him uptight, and he was now a complete sceptic about anything remotely paranormal. I decided to wait until I had evidence.

In the meantime I started my own investigation, writing down all the information Linda had given me. I learned all I could about the land. I checked with Scottish Water to see if the reservoir, called Loch Cote, was still in use. I checked the history of the land using information from an ordnance survey map.

Armed with all these facts I call Neil Robertson, a CID officer, and told him everything. I knew that Linda didn't want to get involved with the police and she was wary of divulging the information to begin with, but I had no other option.

Neil was very understanding when I told him. He arranged for us to go to the area, and we drove to Loch Cote. When he saw it he said that it was the perfect place to kill someone but he could see that this situation was starting to scare me. It was true – I was starting to feel like a nervous wreck. I hardly ate or slept. All I could think about was finding Vicky.

Neil checked the police files and confirmed that the area had been searched already, but that they wanted to speak to Linda themselves before deciding whether or not to search it again. I called Linda several times, but was always told she was out or not available. She never returned any of my calls. I was at a dead end and she had bailed out.

Here I was wading through farmers' mucky fields, searching for drain covers or anything that could hide a body, getting myself worked up only to be dropped by her. I wondered why I had believed her in the first place.

CID wanted to speak to her, but I'd promised I wouldn't involve her without her permission. It was so frustrating. I later found out through a mutual friend that the whole experience had been too much for her. It was another dead end.

*

A few months passed and I hardly ever thought about my dealings with Linda. I had something else to worry about.

The 'family friend' who had abused me as a youngster was coming back to the Falkirk area again. I was devastated. This was a part of my life that I'd tried to forget. I had to cope with the idea I would probably meet him again. That became inevitable when Dad offered to put him and his family up in his house until they found a place of their own. After all these years, he was back in my life, only this time I was a mature adult of 34. I decided to confront this man head-on.

Years ago I'd made it known to members of the family – including Dad – that I never wanted to see this person again. My 'problem' with him was known about in the family, but, as far as I know, never discussed. It was all brushed under the carpet. I'm sure the same sort of 'denial' happens in families everywhere whenever there is a whiff of a scandal.

Dad invited me and Brian to his house shortly after the family friend had moved in. I braced myself when I walked through the door with Brian to be greeted by Dad and Christine, the family friend and his wife. They had all been drinking. The family friend grinned from ear to ear when he saw me, flinging his arms around my neck and hugging me. I gingerly hugged him back. I felt uneasy at his touch. I even felt queasy being in the same room as him. So as not to cause any upset with anyone I put my feelings aside, but I knew from that point on that I would do my best not to be in the same room as him again.

Imagine my surprise when Dad called me, a few days later, asking if I would sing at the birthday party he was organising for the family friend. I tried to give him an excuse for not being able to make it, but he kept going on about how great it would be and that the whole family would be there. I was trying to find the right words to say no.

Then Dad put him on the phone to speak with me. He caught me off guard. I said I would do it, knowing full well that I would later speak to Dad to cancel it. I would leave the explaining to him, even if it meant Dad telling him straight why I wouldn't be there. I put the phone down and wondered whether my dad was expecting me to be buddies with this person. To forgive and forget? He knew how I felt about this man.

I sat and thought it over, but there was no way I could go through with this. I never wanted to see him again. I called Dad and he agreed to come to my house so we could talk. He listened to me as I slowly explained to him why I couldn't and wouldn't sing at that party. I felt nervous talking seriously to him, something I very rarely did. But I had to stick up for myself again, however much I hated confrontation. Dad nodded his head in agreement and said that he understood the situation I had been put in.

After I had finished, he looked at me and asked me whether I would change my mind. I stared at him in disbelief. Had he not heard a word I said? How many times did I have to go through it?

Chapter Nine

I told Dad that I could not visit him while this man was living under his roof, but it didn't stop him from visiting us. I told him I didn't want him to take this matter any further. I wanted to try and forget about it. That was all I was asking for. I felt Dad was disappointed with me, or he was worried. I told him he could make my excuses for me. I never wanted to set eyes on that man again.

I've always enjoyed karaoke and singing and, months later, in August 2005, I had a booking to sing in a pub near Falkirk. Gran was over on holiday from South Africa for a few weeks and I thought it would be nice to take her to my gig with me as she had never seen me perform. I told Dad what I was thinking and he said it would be a fantastic night and he would organise it for Gran to be there. Little did I know that he would also fill a 52-seater bus with family and friends.

I was just about to go on stage in front of my entire family when the family friend walked through the pub door, bold as brass. My heart sank – he was staring straight at me. He is such a cocky person, so over-confident and full of himself.

The old adage that the show must go on was never more true than that night. I burst into song, completely ignoring him a few yards away from me. I felt really proud up there on stage. Although it wasn't *The X Factor*, it had the same stage buzz, and I had achieved my dream. I was performing in front of my family – just like I used to do all these years ago during Mum and Dad's weekend parties. Everyone seemed to be having a great time. Especially the family friend. He was up dancing to most of the songs.

Then, just like a lion stalking its prey, he danced towards me until he was right in front of me as I sang. Taunting me. I struggled to smile as I carried on singing. I noticed Brian watching him closely and he looked concerned. Out of the corner of my eye I could see Lee watching him too. Dad was at the bar and I saw Brian approach him and speak to him. Brian told me later that he had advised my dad to tell the family friend to back off.

Dad obviously decided to ignore Brian's advice, and before I knew it all hell broke loose. Suddenly, right there in front of me the family friend was being punched in the face by Angela's boyfriend, who could see I was upset by this man's attentions. Then Lee started to get involved despite Brian's attempts to restrain him. I was pushed back into my sound equipment. I had just found out I was six weeks pregnant and I lay there clutching my stomach as the mayhem carried on around me.

The next day I called Dad to talk about what had happened. He was immediately dismissive. It didn't take me long to work out that he held me responsible for the fight, because it was my friend's boyfriend who started it. I couldn't understand why I was being blamed. Dad didn't want to discuss it with me and promptly put Christine on the phone. She too sounded furious. She said that my issues with the family friend had nothing to do with my dad, and that I should confront the family friend myself if I had a problem. This was getting out of hand.

She said that what happened between me and the family friend happened years ago and that it should all be left in the past. I wanted to talk to my dad, not her, as I felt it had nothing to do with her, but Christine, as usual, had to put in her tuppence worth. She eventually got me so mad that I put the phone down on her.

That was it. I had had it with Dad and his family. It seemed even more clear to me that he didn't care about me or how I felt. This upset me the most. After all the years of running to my dad, this time I would leave the running to him. Surely he would eventually see my point of view. I would give him a chance to digest what had happened, and maybe he would call me or visit. In the meantime I wasn't going to tell him I was pregnant. He would find out soon enough, but it wasn't going to be from me.

I gave it three months. I never heard from him. I was deeply hurt, confused and angry. It looked as if my own father didn't care for me any more but, being a parent myself, I found that hard to believe. So I wrote him a letter. I told him how I felt and poured my heart out. He didn't reply. I later found out that he had also shown my private letter to other members of the family; rightly or wrongly I felt that my own father was mocking me.

I didn't have the strength to fight him any more, I had my health to look after, now I was carrying my and Brian's baby. I had given him the chance to back me up in a situation that was causing me great anxiety, and he had failed to help me.

A few months later our son John was born. Our initial joy turned to concern as he had to spend the first two weeks of his life in intensive care after inhaling meconium during labour. He was very ill, and Brian and I couldn't even cuddle him. I thought that if Dad was going to contact me, it would be now, because the family jungle drums would have delivered the message that I had given birth. But there was nothing. His grandson was lying in hospital fighting for his life, but still he never called.

I vowed then that my relationship with my father was over. How could I call this man my dad when he failed to take my side against a man he knew had abused me as a child? How could he sit at home when his sick grandson was fighting for his life?

It hurt so badly. To this day I cannot understand his reluctance to meet his grandson. I have many reasons for hating my father now, but when Vicky and I were children he was a fantastic dad, and we were both proud of him.

He always tried to find time to play with Vicky and me

and he always seemed to want to be involved in what we were doing.

For my part, all I wanted now was my father's love and concern for his new grandson. He would never give it to me. But my family troubles paled into insignificance when, just a few months later, the police turned up at my door to tell me they were about to search number 11 Robertson Avenue in Bathgate – and herald the beginning of the end of our search for Vicky.

Chapter Ten

IT WAS WITH a growing sense of revulsion that I watched the breaking news on the television.

It was 4 May 2007, and a man called Peter Tobin had just been found guilty and sent to prison for 21 years for the horrific murder of a Polish student called Angelika Kluk in Glasgow.

Normally I'm not one for watching the news or reading newspapers that much, but the Angelika case had had a huge impact in Scotland, and there was incredible public and press interest on the outcome of his trial. You couldn't avoid becoming fascinated.

It was the images of Tobin, a grey-haired 60-year-old, being led from court that made me sit and stare at the TV, however. As he was being marched handcuffed to the prison van, he lashed out with his feet, kicking a photographer in the throat. His face broke into a terrible snarl. I remember thinking that he looked like a horrible, evil man. It gave me the creeps just catching that glimpse of him before he was driven off to begin his sentence.

Ten minutes later my phone rang. It was Detective Inspector Bert Swanson from Lothian and Borders Police. I knew Bert from the search for Vicky, but he had never been part of the main inquiry team. 'Sharon, are you going to be in? I'd like to pop down and see you for 20 minutes.' I told him I'd be in all day.

About half an hour later Bert turned up at my door accompanied by a female officer. I invited them in, and as they sat down in the living room the news was still on the television.

Nodding towards the television, I said, 'It's terrible what that man did to Angelika Kluk.'

Bert replied solemnly: 'That's why we are here, Sharon.'

Confused, I sat down and listened as Bert revealed that the police had been running a separate inquiry while Tobin was on trial for Angelika Kluk's murder.

'We've been looking at Tobin's background, and in particular where he had been staying,' said Bert. 'And, Sharon, I can tell you that Tobin lived in Bathgate at the time Vicky went missing.'

I just stared at him. Only half an hour before I had been watching Tobin being led away to prison for committing a terrible murder; now I was being told that he lived in the same town where my sister went missing – and at the same time. It was simply unbelievable.

Bert said he couldn't tell me a great deal more as their inquiries were continuing, but he promised to keep in touch. I was so stunned I couldn't speak. Were they trying to tell me that this man could be Vicky's killer?

Just before Bert left, his colleague muttered something about Tobin being 'overlooked' in the past. It didn't quite register with me at the time as I was still shocked at the news Bert had brought, but after they had gone I wondered if Tobin had slipped through the net 16 years earlier. I hadn't seen Tobin before, and until the Angelika case I had never heard his name. It certainly hadn't been mentioned in the inquiry into Vicky. Did the police know about him when Vicky went missing? Was he checked out and allowed to go free? I now wanted all those questions answered.

But I heard nothing for three weeks. It was the most awful wait. I couldn't sleep and spent hours racking my brains. Did Vicky know Tobin? Could she have met him? I didn't think so, but I couldn't be sure. It was torture. All these thoughts and emotions in my head.

I often thought of Mum and wondered what she would have made of all this. She died without any kind of breakthrough in the case. Could we now – over 16 years later – be on the brink of solving my sister's disappearance?

Chapter Ten

Then the police called to warn me they were about to start the search of Tobin's old house in Bathgate because it was inevitable the story would break in the newspapers. The family who now lived there would be moving out to enable officers to search the place from top to bottom and the whole operation could take several weeks to complete.

I was stunned at how quickly things were now moving. Robertson Avenue is less than a mile from the street in Bathgate where Vicky was meant to get on her connecting bus to Falkirk. Could this just be a coincidence? I was due to head off on a holiday to Portugal but I decided before I left that I had to see the house for myself. I just wanted to look at it, I wasn't sure why.

I felt terrible for the family who were about to be forced to move out; for their shock at discovering that someone like Tobin had lived in their home. The police obviously believed that Tobin had been involved in another crime or crimes and that vital evidence could be hidden somewhere in their house.

News of the upcoming search had, as Bert had predicted, broken in the press, so I didn't want to attract any attention by pitching up in front of the house during the day. I knew if there had been any reporters hanging around that day, they would probably have left by the time the light faded, so Brian drove me there late at night, a journey of around ten miles.

I'd never been to Robertson Avenue before. It is in the middle of a maze of streets, and quite hard to find. Eventually we pinpointed the house and parked close enough to see it clearly. Number 11 is an ordinary pebble-dash terraced house, like hundreds of others in Bathgate. It has no real distinguishing features, and it looks directly on to a grassy area.

I am a person who relies very much on instinct, and I hoped if I saw the house I would get some kind of vibe from it. But, as I stared at this rather ordinary-looking building that night, I had no feeling that Vicky's body lay there.

It was the beginning of June 2007 when I headed off for our week's break and I felt very unsettled. I had taken the decision that, despite the activity, it wouldn't help for me to cancel the holiday and stay, but I spent the first couple of days wondering what was going on back in Scotland. I had one phone call from the police to tell me they were about to start the search at the house, then nothing.

When I returned home I realised details of the police operation had been all over the newspapers, although there were no clues as to whether they had found anything. I decided to take another trip up to the Robertson Avenue house. This time Brian's dad drove me, and it was a completely different experience. There was a 'road closed' sign up at the entrance to the street, and a skip was sitting outside the address. I could also just see a police tent that had been erected in the back garden. It looked like a crime scene.

A few days later I had a visit from DCI Keith Anderson. He came to my house and said he wanted to fill me in on some of the details of the search. He said he couldn't tell me too much, but that his officers had removed some 'items' from the house. He didn't tell me what these were, but I knew there must be reasons why he was unable to be specific.

How significant were these items? Had there been a breakthrough? These questions revolved in my head. Keith wasn't giving me the answers I wanted, but I knew he was holding things back for good reason. But after nearly 17 years looking for Vicky I was desperate for any clues.

Within days, some newspapers were reporting that traces of Vicky's DNA had been discovered in the house. Could that be possible after so long? I wondered.

Then, on 21 July, around six weeks after the search at Robertson Avenue had begun, the police at last told me there had been a development. They said Tobin would be charged later that day over Vicky's disappearance. The phrase they used was 'in connection with' Vicky's disappearance.

I was shocked. This was not something I had been

expecting so soon. Keith had told me about the items being removed from the house, and I realised that something had been found, but I didn't expect Tobin to be charged so quickly. I also wondered why, if there was evidence, Tobin hadn't been charged with Vicky's murder. I was completely confused and wrong-footed by this dramatic development.

Again, the police would tell me very little. They kept saying that I was a potential witness and that they couldn't fill me in on the details. I really didn't know what to think. What had the police found in the house? What did 'in connection with' mean? Had Tobin snatched Vicky and then handed her over to someone else? Did this mean she might still be alive? There were so many questions, but few answers.

But it was a positive development. It meant the police believed, and possibly had evidence, that Tobin was involved in Vicky's disappearance in some way.

But, in reality, I knew what this news really meant. I'd read about how Tobin killed Angelika Kluk; how she met a horrific death at the hands of this monster with a string of horrendous previous convictions for similar attacks on young women. I now truly feared my own sister had met a similar fate.

*

I became obsessed by Peter Tobin. The Angelika Kluk trial had grabbed my interest, but now, after he was charged over Vicky's disappearance, it was suddenly much closer to home. There was a growing feeling among the police that this man was definitely responsible for my sister's disappearance. The officers would never tell me anything specific, but there was an air of confidence about the inquiry now which had never existed before. Was it possible the man I had found so abhorrent while I watched that news bulletin that day was Vicky's killer?

The police inquiry began to move at an incredible speed. During the investigations into the Angelika murder, police had secretly launched a separate inquiry called Operation Anagram to look at unsolved disappearances of young women near to where Tobin was known to have lived or travelled.

Letters were sent to all UK police forces urging them to check their missing persons records in relation to Tobin. Initially the response was lukewarm, but some forces took steps to review their old cases.

Following the search of his former home in Bathgate, it became clear through a number of newspaper articles that detectives were visiting other homes he had lived in in the UK, presumably trying to link the dates of occupancy with the last sightings of any women who had gone missing in the area.

Tobin's known addresses since the 1960s included three properties in Brighton, two in Scotland (including the house in Bathgate) and two in Hampshire – one in Southsea and another in Havant – and at least one property in Margate in Kent. The house in Southsea was searched in September, and details made the news.

I remember reading about the Southsea search and thinking: 'Could Vicky have been there?' But I dismissed those thoughts quickly. It was so far away. I simply believed the police were being thorough and doing what they had to do.

After detectives had told me that Vicky's body hadn't been discovered in the Bathgate house, I believed she would probably never be found. I never really contemplated for a minute that the police would stumble upon my sister's body somewhere in England. If the Bathgate house was the possible link to Vicky and she wasn't there, I held out little hope of finding her dead … or alive.

*

After the search at Robertson Avenue ended, there was a great deal of speculation in the media about what the police had found in the house. The story was everywhere, in the papers and on the TV. And I came under a lot of pressure to speak to the media – all of which I resisted. I wanted to wait and see what happened before making any kind of statement.

But my father, desperate to be involved in some way, just couldn't help himself. I discovered that he had been pictured outside the Bathgate house while the search was going on saying that he hoped Vicky would be found.

Shortly after the search ended the *Daily Record* reported that DNA traces from Vicky had been found in the house. Another paper reported that police had found a knife. There was no confirmation and at the time I didn't know what to believe.

Everything, however, seemed to point towards Tobin's involvement in Vicky's disappearance, and I got the distinct impression that police were working towards charging him with her murder, despite the fact there was no body.

Things moved quickly after the initial Bathgate search, and within a few weeks police were visiting other homes Tobin had lived in, including the one in Portsmouth in October.

But suddenly, almost as if they were acting on definite information, in late autumn the police emphasis shifted to Tobin's old house in Margate. Officers immediately began digging up the garden while initially leaving the house itself intact.

It later transpired they believed that if remains were

found there, they would belong to another young girl who had been missing for some time. I don't know what led them to believe this, but that was the line of inquiry they were following.

Then, on 12 November 2007, officers digging below the sandpit came upon some bones and clothing …

It wasn't the girl they were expecting. It was Vicky.

Two days later police arrived at my door to deliver the news.

The following day Tobin, who had only been charged in connection with Vicky's disappearance back in July, appeared in court officially charged with her murder.

Chapter Eleven

I HAD ALWAYS hoped that if Vicky was ever found it would bring my father and me closer together; that something so tragic would put things in perspective and make our family differences appear trivial. I was so wrong. It did the exact opposite. From the day the police uncovered Vicky's body, the enormity of the situation seemed to amplify our already fractured relationship and drive an even bigger and ultimately more public wedge between us.

On many occasions over the years, Vicky had acted as the go-between as far as Dad and I were concerned. She was often the peacemaker when he and I had fallen out, and it was usually through her that I maintained some kind of relationship with Dad during the difficult times. Now, through the tragic circumstances of her death, I hoped that Dad and I could face this together. It is exactly what Vicky would have wanted. Sadly, it wasn't to be.

The story of what happened in the aftermath of us finding out that Vicky had been murdered and dumped in a hole in the ground for almost 17 years is itself a tragedy. A sorry story of hate, betrayal and crocodile tears played out in front of millions of people.

After learning that Vicky's body had been found, I had to try to begin to come to terms with finding out that, as I had suspected for many years, Vicky had been brutally murdered. It was all over the news, as were pictures of the excavated garden at the house in Margate where poor Vicky had been unceremoniously dumped. An article in one newspaper said that Tobin's young son had played in a sandpit in the garden, which lay above where Vicky's body was. Tobin actually let him play there, knowing what lay in the dark earth just a few feet underneath his son's feet. My mind was full of new questions those first few days. How did Vicky get to Margate? Did she die the night she was abducted? Did Tobin keep her a prisoner in Bathgate and then move her while she was still alive? I hoped with all my heart that when he did kill her it was quick and she wasn't tortured and didn't suffer.

Later I phoned DCI Keith Anderson and told him that I wanted to travel to Margate and lay flowers for Vicky over the weekend. But Keith strongly advised against the idea, because of the media attention it would cause. Instead he suggested he personally organise everything for me and he would have officers lay the flowers on our behalf. He took out his mobile and arranged it there and then. So the very next day our flowers were put on the spot where Vicky had lain for nearly 17 years. The CID even took photographs of the flowers and sent me copies.

Around that time, I received a conciliatory text message from my half-sister Kirsty. She believed something as important as this should bring Dad and me closer together. She said that he needed all the support he could get and suggested that I go to his house, walk through his door and give him a cuddle. She claimed that he would welcome me with open arms.

Since she was well aware of why I hadn't spoken to my father for months and she knew all about the incident with the family friend, her text was asking a great deal of me. I recognised that Dad and I needed to talk about Vicky, but I wasn't backing down as easily as that. I was determined I wasn't going to do all the running.

After a great deal of thought, I sent a reply stating that I would meet him halfway. It was the best I could do. However, she told me that that wasn't an option; Dad and Christine wouldn't entertain that idea. I remember thinking that this wasn't about Christine; it was about the relationship I had with my father. Could my dad not speak for himself? I felt it was time that Christine kept her nose out of my business with Dad. I took a decision to make contact with Dad; there was no avoiding it. I had to speak to him about Vicky and that was too important for this family feud to continue.

The police told me that Peter Tobin would be appearing at the court in Linlithgow, about ten miles from Falkirk, the next day. I asked if I could go to the court to see face to face the man who I was now sure had killed Vicky. They told me they couldn't stop me, but that they didn't think it was a good idea. They said the press would turn out in huge numbers and I'd be putting myself in the spotlight by being there.

They also told me it was just a procedural hearing in front of a sheriff only and that the public would not be allowed into court. I decided not to go; instead I put my faith in our justice system. I knew that one day in the not-too-distant future I would look Vicky's killer in the eye and hopefully see him sent to prison for a very long time.

The day of Tobin's court appearance I picked up the phone and dialled Dad's mobile number, but he didn't pick up. Lindsay was with me, so we waited a while and I got her to call him from her mobile, so he wouldn't recognise the number. Sure enough, he answered. Lindsay said who she was and that I wanted to speak with him. He barked back that he was at Linlithgow Sheriff Court for Tobin's court case and he didn't want to speak to me.

I immediately switched on the TV and tuned in to the news. I couldn't believe what I saw. There was Dad walking in front of the prison van that contained Peter Tobin, leading it into the court car park. Beside him were members of his family and they were walking just like they were in a funeral procession. The police didn't stop him, and I could hear the photographers busily clicking away.

What the hell was he playing at? The press would have a field day. There was my father posturing in front of the van carrying Tobin as if he'd been found guilty already. He was risking everything. If he wanted justice for Vicky he was going the wrong way about it.

I couldn't understand what Dad was playing at. Dad is many things, but he is not stupid. I knew there would be a multitude of emotions going through his head; it was a traumatic time for everyone. I also knew how much he loved Vicky – he showed it on countless occasions when we were young – and I knew how much it meant for him to get justice for her death.

As I watched him on the television I admit I did feel sympathy for him. No parent should have to go through what he and Mum went through after Vicky disappeared. But I was also seething. I wanted to call him straight away and tell him to stop, but I waited until the van had disappeared inside the court grounds. Lindsay dialled his number and Christine answered. I could hear how excited she was. She told Lindsay they were at a coffee shop across from the court and that Dad was too upset to speak on the phone. She said they had just seen Tobin going into court and Dad had been shouting at him and calling him a murdering bastard.

I was so shocked at what Christine was saying but I was powerless to do anything about it. As much as I too believed now that Tobin had probably killed Vicky, Dad wasn't doing anyone any good by making a fool of himself in front of the world's media before Tobin was convicted. Whatever happened to dignity?

Lindsay took the opportunity to ask Christine if Dad had made any arrangements for Vicky's funeral as police had said they hoped to release her body to the family soon. I could hear Christine getting animated again on the other end of the line and I could see Lindsay getting angrier and angrier. Christine had pompously told her that the funeral arrangements would be made and that she would be told about them soon. Dad was apparently thinking about burying Vicky beside Mum, but whatever decision he made, Christine told Lindsay, we would get a phone call telling us the day and time and where the funeral would be. So Christine had decreed that the funeral was nothing to do with us. But when Lindsay had questioned her further Christine cut the connection. I was annoyed that we appeared to be being pushed aside. But I realised that being angry wasn't going to get me anywhere with Dad, especially as he had Christine as his guard dog. They were holding the higher hand and I think they both enjoyed the effect it was having on us.

Once I'd calmed down sufficiently I sent a text message to Dad saying that we should put our differences aside as there were more important things to discuss. He never replied.

It was obvious that Dad was not in a state of mind to give a statement to the press, so his brother Eric did his talking for him. He was quoted saying that Dad was 'happy that the long road might nearly be at an end now'. That was true – we were coming to an end to one of Britain's longest-running juvenile disappearances – but we hadn't finished our journey just yet. We still had the trial to endure. That's when we would find out what really happened. And it was something that I was dreading.

I tried to phone Dad a couple of times after Tobin's court appearance, but he ignored my calls. My mother's words kept popping into my head; the warning she'd given to Uncle Ian on her deathbed – that Dad would try and take over if Vicky's body was found. I knew from the resounding silence that this was happening behind my back. The very thought tore at my heart; to think that we might be ignored when such important matters were being decided. We had all waited so long to lay Vicky to rest, and now Dad was taking over.

To my mind it didn't matter how much my dad dressed it up, despite those happy early years in my opinion he let Vicky down too often. He had walked out on her all those years ago without a backward glance. The twins and I were Vicky's real family, the one she was brought up with. I made a pledge with myself that I was going to do all I could to get custody of Vicky's remains. She had to be laid to rest properly. And I had a right to make it happen.

Dad had been quoted in the newspapers saying that he was planning Vicky's funeral for after Christmas, so my immediate concern was allayed. Nothing was going to happen for a month or so. Also, the police had told me that they were carrying out toxicology tests on Vicky's spleen and other examinations on her voice box; so having the funeral after Christmas would allow time for this.

The events of the last few days had taken their toll on me and I felt terrible, so bad I went to the doctor. I was finding it very hard to cope, looking after John and Emma-Jane, supporting the twins and worrying about what was going through Dad's head. He diagnosed stress and gave me some tablets to keep me calm. I felt like I was on the edge of a nervous breakdown, but something inside me would not let me weaken. I had to be strong. Dad wouldn't talk to me and I couldn't understand why. What was he afraid of? I was his daughter, and, unlike poor Vicky, I was still here.

Five days after Vicky's body was found, Dad finally

called me. I picked up my mobile and spoke to him for the first time in nearly two years. There were no pleasantries. He simply said he was buying two burial plots in the Grand Sable Cemetery near his home in Redding. He told me that Vicky would be laid to rest there with him because it was near the place where she'd grown up. I was stunned. Why had he chosen there? I immediately told him about Mum's dying wish that she be buried beside her. He simply said: 'She never told me that.'

I could tell by the tone of his voice that his mind was made up. I made it clear that I wasn't happy with his decision and that I thought it was wrong. If the roles had been reversed and it was he who had died and Mum who was alive, then she would have buried Vicky beside him.

I was heartbroken, not for me but for Vicky and my mum. After 17 years lying in the ground 400 miles away from home, Vicky's final resting place should be beside her mother. How could Dad be so cruel and selfish? He was carrying a family grudge to ridiculous extremes and I was determined to fight him all the way. This was my mum's last wish, and I would move mountains to make sure it was fulfilled.

I decided to make an appointment with the procurator fiscal whose office was responsible for liaising with the Crown Prosecution Service in England about releasing Vicky's body for burial. I wanted to stake my claim for joint custody of Vicky's remains, which might afford me legal rights in the decision about where she would be buried.

So I prepared myself with all the information I needed to try and help me get her back. My argument would be that Dad had left Vicky when she was very young and that he didn't have a lot to do with her upbringing. Mum and Dad divorced back in 1985, but they'd had a chaotic relationship before that, with Dad bouncing between Christine and Mum for years. What gave him the right to decide something as important as this?

I also took the decision to speak to the press. If Dad wouldn't hear me out, then I would let him read about it. I wanted Dad to respect Mum's last wishes – and to respect Vicky – and I was ready to shout about it in a bid to make him see sense.

Lindsay had a good relationship with a reporter from the *Falkirk Herald,* so she arranged for him to come to our house for an interview. We told him we wanted to express our thanks and gratitude to the local people of Falkirk and the surrounding area, who had sympathised with our family, and also to the police for their hard work and determination. But we also made it clear in the article that we were against my father's plans to bury Vicky at Grand Sable and that we would fight him all the way to fulfil our mother's wish.

The article in the *Herald* was picked up by the national

press in a way I could never have imagined. FAMILY AT WAR screamed the headlines. I was astonished at the reaction and I had a procession of reporters at my door. I sent them all away, with the information that I had said all I wanted to say in my local paper.

My interview obviously angered Dad too, and all hope that he would see sense over the funeral disappeared when I picked up a copy of the *Sun* the next day where he made it abundantly clear that he would carry on with his plans and attacked me for interfering. He also begged for sympathy from the public because his little girl had been murdered.

I was livid and hit back in an interview with the *Scottish Daily Mail* accusing Dad of abandoning his family. The whole row was spiralling out of control, and what should have been a private family matter was now a very public, media one. But I felt I had to do this for Mum and Vicky.

The next day I had my appointment with the procurator fiscal. The twins and Brian came with me to give their support. I was very nervous, but I knew I had to do this. I felt positive that I had a strong argument. We were due to meet CID officer Pat Gaughan at the office in Edinburgh but while we were on the way there Pat called me on my mobile. He sounded as if he was dreading making the call to me. He told me he had just been to Dad's house and delivered Vicky's death certificate to him.

I knew what this meant. Dad only needed the certificate to allow him to go ahead with the funeral. I felt I'd had the rug whipped from under my feet. How could this have happened so quickly? Just as I was preparing to fight with Dad about the funeral, he had managed somehow to get Vicky's death certificate and, presumably, a promise from the Crown Prosecution Service that her body would be released to him soon.

When we arrived I was still numb and trying to digest the news I'd just been given. Pat could hardly look me in the eye. He knew how much this meant to me, but he had only been doing his job. Dad had applied for the certificate as next of kin, and the police had no real alternative but to give it to him.

But there was another bombshell waiting. The procurator fiscal told me she had released Vicky's body to Dad. I just stared at her. I couldn't believe what she had just said. Here I was preparing to fight for custody of Vicky, and she'd already given her to Dad. It was a fait accompli. She must have seen the look of horror on my face, and she asked me what was wrong. I explained why I'd come to see her; she had had no idea that I wanted custody of Vicky.

She was very sympathetic, but the damage was done. She was talking to me, but I wasn't listening or taking anything in. My mind was too busy processing the bad news. Two devastating blows in the space of an hour.

Now I knew I could do nothing legally to stop the funeral plans, I had no alternative but to throw myself at my father's mercy. I had to make him see that Vicky should be beside her mother. I had to speak to him again.

On Sunday, 25 November, I prepared to call Dad. I'd worked out what I was going to say to him.

Dad answered immediately. I was surprised when he told me he was in Margate. I asked him politely when it would be possible to meet up with him so the twins and I could discuss our part in Vicky's funeral.

'What has it to do with the twins?' he barked back at me. I gasped; I wondered if I'd heard him correctly.

'They are Vicky's brother and sister,' I said. 'They have a right to be involved.'

'What about *my* children?' he said.

I could tell this was about to turn nasty, so I said: 'Okay. Can you and I meet to talk?' To my surprise he agreed and we arranged to meet when he returned from Margate.

Later that day Dad was on every single news channel. He wasn't in Margate on his own. He'd taken along Christine, his brother Eric and an entourage of other family members. They'd all travelled en masse to see Vicky's final resting place and the media were there to witness it.

I watched as Eric's son, a serving soldier, saluted her shallow grave, while Dad spoke to the reporters with tears in his eyes. He was telling the world how he'd searched for his daughter for 17 years, and now he'd found her.

On Tuesday, 27 November my mobile rang early and Dad's number flashed up on screen. I'd been waiting for his call so we could make our final arrangements to meet. His tone was very matter-of-fact. 'Vicky's funeral will be on Friday at Redding Church. She will be buried at Grand Sable Cemetery.'

I was stunned into silence. I wanted to scream at him, but the words wouldn't come. He'd gone ahead and arranged Vicky's funeral behind my back. I was so surprised all I could muster was a question about flowers and funeral cars. Then he put the phone down on me.

I burst into tears. How could he have done this to me and the twins; to Vicky's own mother? Although he said her roots were in Redding and that he wanted her buried there as quickly as possible so he could put the matter behind him, I couldn't help but feel that he had brought forward the funeral to before Christmas to stop me persuading the authorities to bury her with her mother.

He had denied my mother her dying wish. No matter what their differences were when she was alive, there was love there at one time. Now he had delivered the final insult to the woman who nurtured Vicky, the woman who wiped away her tears and fears and raised her.

And I felt so sorry for Vicky. In the whole public row about her remains and funeral, it was almost as if she had been sidelined. If she could have witnessed what was happening – her family fighting among themselves – she would have been distraught. She would have hated this, and I despised myself for getting involved, but the way I saw it, I had little choice.

It broke my heart that Vicky would be buried alone in a plot that would one day hold my father's body – and probably Christine's. It was unforgivable. Vicky deserved to be in peace next to her mother, not Christine. Now Mum wasn't here to defend us. I was alone. Alone in the thoughts that there was nothing that I could do to change his mind.

Now I knew that I had reached the end of the road in my battle to have Vicky buried beside Mum. There was nothing else I could do. He had won. I had to compose myself and prepare for my little sister's funeral. I told myself that I had to act with dignity and do nothing to taint Vicky's memory.

Dad called me again later that day; this time to tell me that Vicky's coffin would arrive at the funeral directors the following day. He sounded so distant, but I bit my tongue and listened to what he had to say. He said that if I wanted to go and pay my last respects to Vicky in private then I should make an appointment with the parlour. I thanked him for telling me and put the phone down.

I spoke to the twins, and Lindsay said she wanted to go with me. We made an arrangement for the next day. Brian suggested that I write a letter to Vicky and take a photograph to place in her coffin. I thought it was a lovely idea, so I sat that night and wrote a letter to my dead sister. I thanked her for being my little sister and said I was sorry I hadn't managed to look after her properly the night she disappeared, but most of what I wrote will remain a secret. I do not want anything to taint the message I wrote to her straight from the heart.

When I'd finished the tears were rolling down my cheeks. The funeral my dad had arranged was his send-off, what he felt he needed to do. I'd said my goodbyes in that note. This was between me and my sister.

We reached the funeral parlour as the flowers were arriving for Vicky's funeral. They were beautiful, and their aroma filled the small vestry. When I saw them, it all started to hit me. These were for *my* sister, and she lay dead in the next room.

We had been separated for 17 years, and now we were together in the same place. I'd spent so long searching. Years of worry and not knowing. Now I would be with Vicky again.

A member of staff led us to another room. I held my breath as I walked in. Vicky's light oak coffin lay under two dim wall lamps, the brass handles gleaming in the light. There was one chair in the room. I sat down. There she was in front of me. My sister and me separated by a simple wooden frame. I read the brass plaque on the lid: Vicky Faye Hamilton.

I took out the envelope from my bag. It contained my note to Vicky and some photographs of the two of us as children. I leaned over and placed the note on top of her coffin and whispered: 'I love you, Vicky. I never gave up searching for you and I missed you every day. I'm glad you are home with me now.'

I told her that I was sorry that I wasn't able to lay her to rest beside Mum.

And there in that solemn room I spoke to my sister again after 17 years. I said goodbye and told her I would always love her.

*

That day the Reverend Jeff Smart, the minister who was due to conduct the ceremony, also came to see me. He was a lovely man and I warmed to him as soon as I met him. He was grey-haired, tall and slim, and wore spectacles perched on the end of his nose. He explained to me what was going to happen at the funeral and what hymns would be sung.

His office had been inundated with the media calling asking if they could have permission to set up camera equipment in his church, but he said he had declined all their requests. I was relieved to hear him say that – the last thing that I wanted was cameras in my face. Because of the nature of this funeral and the public's interest he was, however, considering allowing one camera in to record the event for news purposes.

It had been years since I had been in Redding Church. Vicky and I used to go to Sunday school there when we were very young. I knew they had an adjoining building extended onto the back of the church and luckily it was still there because it was going to be used as an overspill area for the public and the press.

Reverend Smart asked me if I wanted to say a few words during the service, but I decided not to. I wasn't sure if I'd be able to cope with the stress of standing up in front of so many people.

*

Friday 30 November – the day of my sister's funeral. I had a long-standing dental appointment that morning which I purposely didn't cancel. I wanted to go somewhere where I could take my mind off the events of the day. I needed some personal space to try and compose myself. I was determined to get through this with my dignity intact.

Dad had called with a softer tone in his voice to ask if the twins and I wanted a table reserved at his local pub the

Callendar Arms for after the funeral. I told him we'd made our own arrangements. I wanted our wake to be for friends and family; I knew Dad wanted his to be more public.

When I got back home the house was filled with people. Both Brian's family and my family were there. Here to support us all. Brian's sister Elizabeth were going to stay behind to look after John and Emma-Jane.

I took Lee and Lindsay outside for a quiet word. We were all nervous, and I told them that today would be hard but we would all get through it, together. I said that we all had to act with dignity and respect.

We had to rise above the family bickering for Vicky's sake. This was her day. I told them that I was proud of them both and that if Mum was here today she would say the same.

'We'll get through this together,' I said. We then all hugged, and I gave them each a single red rose.

The twins were adults now, but that day they looked so vulnerable. The early days of Vicky's disappearance passed them by. They were just six years old, and simply didn't understand. But I remember how much they meant to Vicky; how much she loved them. She spent ages playing with them, especially with Lindsay. She made time to take them to the swing park, and loved nothing better than dressing the pair of them up to take them out.

The twins were robbed of growing up with their sister.

Tragically, that day, they would finally say goodbye to a girl who they had been only truly getting to know before she disappeared.

The funeral car arrived ten minutes early and the sight of it brought me back down to earth. I told Brian that I wasn't ready to go and needed a few more minutes to compose myself. I took a few dep breaths. This was it. I would do this for Mum and Vicky.

Brian, Lindsay and her partner David, Lee with his partner Charlene and I climbed into the car. My heart was pounding. Brian gripped my hand and winked at me, which made me smile. The car drove slowly on the three-mile journey to Redding Church.

When we turned into Main Street the roads were lined with parked cars, all the way down the street and past the church. I had walked up and down this road so many times as I grew up, but had never seen it so busy.

Just as we pulled up to the church I could see the media standing four deep at the side of the road. They were in people's gardens, on top of walls, up on van roofs. It was chaotic. Then I saw Dad's car pull up behind us and I turned to Brian: 'Let Dad go in first.' It was a miserable day and the rain was lashing down as I watched Dad, Christine and their entourage disappear through the church door.

Now it was our turn. I braced myself as I stepped out of the car to the sound of cameras clicking. I kept my head held high. I had nothing to be ashamed of. On climbing the few steps up to the church I could see hordes of people, but I just stared straight ahead, not engaging with anyone. I just wanted to get into the church and to my seat as fast as I could.

Reverend Smart greeted us at the church doors, and showed me where we should sit. I could hardly get past the crowds of people jammed into the back of the church, but they all moved when they saw us walk in.

As I followed Reverend Smart down the aisle I looked up and saw the back of Christine's head. She was sitting on the left-hand side at the front next to Dad. As I took my seat on the right-hand side of the church, I looked up and saw a dozen or so reporters and cameramen seated in the pews to my right. So much for no press inside the church.

To the left and in front of me lay Vicky's coffin.

So many people connected to Vicky's life were in the church that day to pay their respects: her teachers from school; the police officers who searched for her; Mum's old neighbours; Vicky's old schoolfriends – all there to remember a vibrant, wonderful girl.

As I looked across at her coffin with its beautiful array of flowers, I realised that one thing was missing: a picture of Vicky. I wished Dad had thought of putting her photograph on top of her coffin for everyone to see and to remember the beautiful girl she had been.

I sat with my head bowed, thinking of my little sister. I tried not to look over at where Dad was sitting. I'm not quite sure how I got through the service, and I can remember very little about the sermon except Reverend Smart talking about an 'act of evil' which had brought Vicky here today, back home to Redding. I just wanted this to end and I squeezed Brian's arm trying to find comfort and security.

After the service I emerged from the church to face what seemed like an even larger group of reporters and photographers. As my uncle John led me to our waiting car I caught Kirsty's eye and mouthed the words, 'Are you okay?' She nodded her head and dropped her gaze.

We stood waiting until the funeral directors had placed Vicky's coffin into the back of the hearse. I felt uneasy standing so close to Dad and Christine, but I stayed with Brian and said nothing to them.

I couldn't believe that our family had disintegrated to such an extent that we were standing beside Vicky's coffin and we couldn't even bring ourselves to talk to each other. How had things got so bad? Vicky meant so much to all of us, especially Dad. He doted on her when she was young. He was obviously heartbroken, but I just couldn't bring myself to forgive him, even on the day of Vicky's funeral, for his decision to bury her at Grand Sable.

My mind went back to when Vicky and I were young

and Mum and Dad were happy together: Vicky running about with what seemed endless energy, and me, more reserved, trying to get her to settle down and play with our dolls. They were happy, family days. Good times that I will never forget.

Strangely, on one of the saddest days of my life, memories of one of the happiest came into my head. It was the summer of 1977, when I was only six years old, and it was shortly before my father's affair became public. It was a brilliantly sunny day and Vicky and I were in our back garden where Mum and Christine had built us makeshift tents using bedsheets draped over a washing line. We played for hours in our little hideaway.

How had we now come to this situation? A family once so united stood together in physical form, but, in reality, had never been so fragmented; we stood in the miserable pouring rain waiting to bury my sister, my father's little daughter. It was so, so painfully sad.

Vicky's hearse went in front with the funeral director walking beside it, leading the procession. Dad's car slowly followed it and ours followed his down the hill to the nearby cemetery.

I had made one request of Dad before the funeral, and that was to allow the cortege to drive past our old home in Ward Avenue. To my surprise, he had agreed. So now, 17 years after she left it Vicky was finally making it home.

As our car passed the house where Vicky, Mum, the twins and I were a family I allowed myself a smile as the tears rolled down my cheeks. There were happy times in that house. The times I spent as Vicky's big sister. Nobody could take that away. And now Vicky was home at last.

As we drove into the cemetery I was astounded to see so many people, considering we were the first ones out of the church. The place was crawling with press. I could see them running to get up ahead of our cars so they could get their cameras ready.

When we parked I sat in the car. I didn't know what would happen next. We sat for about five minutes, watching all the faces gather round the plot that Dad had chosen for Vicky. People huddled under umbrellas as the rain fell relentlessly. Finally we got out the car. I kept my head down, not wanting to make eye contact with anyone as we squeezed through the crowd.

It was like a funeral scene from an old black-and-white horror movie. Although it was late morning, the sky was so dark it seemed like early evening. The sky was slate grey, and the rain fell as if it would never stop.

I looked around at the other mourners, most of whom had trudged up the hill from the huge car park to the elevated graveyard. Most carried umbrellas; many looked soaked to the skin. It was a miserable scene.

Although it was a sizeable graveyard, I could see

people gathered around Vicky's grave about four rows in from some cemetery outbuildings. They were all standing huddled together, bracing themselves against the driving rain.

There must have been over 200 people at the church for the service, and it looked as if most had travelled the mile down the road to the graveyard. I walked forward onto the grass and felt the ground squelch under my feet. I didn't care. As I got closer to the front I could see a carpet of flowers in the distance which seemed to go on for ever.

Finally we approached the plot. Dad and his family stood to the right of us. I stared straight ahead and saw the press lined up against the cemetery wall. I gripped Brian's hand and he leaned into me and softly kissed my head.

The undertaker asked for the cord holders to move forward as he read out their numbers. Lee and I had agreed that we wanted to be assigned cords; Lindsay said she couldn't face taking one. I'd told Dad this earlier in the week and he seemed surprised. But I was determined to have my place – at number two cord, for Mum and me – and Lee had every right to his. He'd first had this responsibility at the age of eight for his mother's coffin; now he'd do it again at 23 for his sister's.

The undertaker called for number one cord holder. Dad stepped forward. Up until this point Dad and I hadn't looked each other's way during the funeral. Now he stood just yards in front of me, his head bowed, staring down at Vicky's coffin.

I didn't take my eyes off him. I just glared at him, thinking: 'This is wrong and he knows it.' He kept his head down. I continued to stare as the undertaker called for the other cord holders to come forward. Finally Dad looked up. Our eyes locked and I gave him a look of pure disappointment and betrayal; the look my mother would have given him had she been there. He shifted uneasily as he lowered his eyes to the ground again.

The undertaker brought me back to reality when he asked me gently not to wind the cord around my gloved hands, joking that he didn't want to have to fish me out of the grave. I smiled at him as I unravelled the rope.

We all said a prayer before we lowered Vicky into the ground. I blew Vicky a kiss and threw a rose into the grave as I turned away. I had said my private goodbyes in a better place. This was not where Vicky should be, and I wanted to leave.

Dad was crying his eyes out as I turned away from the graveside, but I had little sympathy for him.

*

Vicky's funeral had two wakes, such was the division within our family.

I gathered with Vicky's old friends and my family in a

local bowling club. Dad went to the pub. I found it heart-warming to hear Vicky's name mentioned every time I passed a table. I made a short speech in which I thanked everyone for coming and said that I'd done everything humanly possible to get Dad to bury Vicky beside her mum and that I was sorry that I'd failed. The people in the room groaned. But I didn't want anybody sitting moping about that, instead I wanted them to all celebrate the life Vicky lived. 'I count my blessings every day that I was lucky enough to know her,' I said.

Everybody in the room clapped, and I felt proud that I'd managed to get through the day. Before the funeral I had managed to put together a photo album of pictures, images of Vicky, Mum, Vicky's friends, and some family members. Pictures of Vicky smiling. Happy times. I watched it being passed around the hall filled with the people who really loved Vicky.

Later that evening our doorbell rang. Brian answered it. It was a reporter from the *Sun*. I overheard the man asking if I wanted to make a comment on the hand gesture I had given to Dad that day at the burial. Brian said he didn't know what he was talking about. But the reporter told Brian that a photo had landed on his desk earlier, which showed me making a V-sign to my dad.

When Brian came back in, he asked me outright, with a smile on his face, whether I had made a V-sign to my dad. I told him I hadn't. The next day's headlines in the *Sun* read: V FOR VICKY. When I saw the picture of me with my hand in the V shape, it was clear to me I was unravelling the cord at the graveside as the undertaker had told me to do. I would never have shown disrespect to my dead sister by doing something like that over her grave. But part of me didn't care what people believed; I knew the truth.

Vicky would be up there laughing at this, I thought.

*

To this day, my father and I haven't spoken again.

I fought for 17 years to bring my sister back home, and I did my bit to achieve that. I will never ever forgive him for refusing to carry out my mother's dying wish. He could at least have given his family – and especially Vicky – that. Now that same family would have to face another severe test – one of the hardest – to confront the man accused of killing Vicky across a courtroom.

Chapter Twelve

SITTING IN THE drab and soulless confines of the witness room where I had been waiting for two long days, I froze as I heard the court official call out my name. This was it, the moment I had been dreading for so long. It was my turn to give evidence. My opportunity to tell my story in a court of law.

I'd gone over and over in my head what I would say. For weeks before I'd tried to guess the questions I would be asked. Now, with the official's voice ringing in my ears, I'd suddenly forgotten everything I'd mentally rehearsed. My head was filled with just one thought. I was about to come face to face with Peter Tobin, the man who I believed had murdered my little sister.

I stood up, and with reassuring words from Brian, Lindsay and my friend Angela who had all been waiting with me, I followed the official out of the room, along the short corridor to the main courtroom. I paused at the door. I was sweating and shaking and my heart was racing.

The court official asked me if I was ready and I took a deep breath before entering the room. I stared straight ahead, but I didn't take anything in. It was as if I had tunnel vision as I walked into the witness box. I let out a gasp which I felt must have been heard by the whole courtroom.

I knew in my mind's eye where everyone should be sitting as I'd been taken on a pre-trial tour of the building by officials from the Crown Office two weeks earlier. I looked directly ahead and saw the familiar face of Frank Mulholland, the kindly lawyer who was leading the prosecution case. He gave me a half smile and I immediately felt relief. It was going to be all right. Frank was there in front of me.

I knew I had to concentrate on Frank if I was to get through these first few minutes without crumbling. But I knew I couldn't put off the inevitable any longer. I knew *he* was sitting in the dock of the court. I had to look at him. I had to look at Peter Tobin.

This was the moment I'd thought about so much, coming face to face with the man who snatched Vicky. I knew he still had to be convicted, but everything pointed towards him being responsible for Vicky's disappearance. Her body had been found in the garden of his old house. How could he explain that?

I knew exactly where he would be sitting. My eyes flitted to my left. I saw a tiny figure, almost hunched, sitting between two guards. It was *him*. It was Tobin. After 17 years I was in the same room as the man accused of Vicky's murder. Seventeen years searching for an answer to her disappearance and now, as I took in his pathetic figure, I believed the answer was sitting in front of me.

As I looked towards him his eyes were fixed on the ground in front of him. He was wearing a pastel-coloured sweater, which seemed out of kilter with the rest of the solemn surroundings.

When he finally looked up I saw him more clearly: a wizened, wiry man, almost pathetic. But his eyes told a different story. They were weasel-like. And they were cold and dead. I looked away in disgust. I had seen Tobin. Now I wanted to get on with the business of getting justice for my murdered sister...

*

Weeks before Tobin's trial was due to take place at the High Court in Dundee I was called to a meeting at the Crown Office in Edinburgh. An official had told me on the phone that they wanted to explain the details of the charges facing Tobin before they were released to the press. They warned me that I might find some of the details upsetting.

When I arrived at the offices I was shown into a room and after a brief chat – and another warning about what I was about to read – I was handed a piece of paper.

By this time I was almost scared to look at the document, but I knew I had to. Nothing could have prepared me for what was written there.

The words jumped out at me. Abduction. Murder. Drugs. Sexual assault. I felt the tears coming. I just couldn't take it in properly. This is what happened to Vicky? I composed myself and read the charge properly.

Tobin was accused of abducting and murdering Vicky and also attempting to defeat the ends of justice. The charges alleged that on 11 February 1991, in Bathgate, West Lothian, Tobin abducted Vicky, took her to his home in Robertson Avenue, and there, or elsewhere, drugged her, caused an injury to her neck during a struggle, committed a sexual assault and murdered her.

Between then and 15 December 1991 in Bathgate, Edinburgh and Margate, it was alleged Tobin did a number of things to prevent Vicky's body being found. The charge alleged that Vicky's body was hidden and that Tobin disposed of her clothing, footwear and belongings.

Then, knowing police were conducting a missing person's inquiry, Tobin was charged with putting Vicky's purse under a portable cabin in a bid to mislead police into believing she had run away from home.

Then I read the words that still chill me to this day. I was so shocked I felt myself go weak.

The charge went on to allege that Tobin cut Vicky's body

in two with knives, wrapped her in bin bags, hid the knives and concealed, transported and buried the body parts.

Cut her body in two. This was too much to take. I dropped the sheet of paper and burst into tears. I knew deep down that Vicky must have suffered a terrible ordeal, but this was just too horrific. My poor sister had fallen prey to a man who, if these charges were proved, was nothing short of a monster.

*

Now I stood in front of this monster sitting meekly in the dock. Still he refused to acknowledge me. I looked up at Frank and got ready to take the oath. As the judge asked me to solemnly swear to tell the truth I thought of Vicky and my dear mother. I thanked God that she was not here to witness this. She couldn't have handled it.

In his gentle voice Frank began to ask me questions. Simple questions to begin with before he moved on to ask me about the last weekend Vicky and I spent together – the weekend she went missing.

I've told the story of our final weekend so many times it is seared into my brain. I've analysed every detail over the last 17 years time and time again. Yet in the atmosphere of the court I felt very emotional and vulnerable. I was scared to make a mistake; to get some fact or other wrong. I felt the tears building up and I felt as if I was about to crack.

Frank asked me if I had said farewell to Vicky as she waited for the bus to take her home.

'Yes,' I replied. 'We hugged each other. I watched the bus drive away.'

I was then asked what life had been like for me and my family since that evening. I said: 'It has been a 17-year nightmare.'

Frank then asked me to look at jewellery and clothing, which had been found with a body at an address in Margate in Kent in November the previous year. I looked at them. They were the clothes and jewellery Vicky had been wearing the night she got the bus home. It was heartbreaking to look at them. Vicky had borrowed them from our mother to wear that weekend. Mum had joked that she had gone away with 'half her jewellery'.

Then the courtroom was shown the last picture taken of Vicky, at Christmas two months before she disappeared. The image was projected onto screens in the court. I could see the black onyx ring she wore. When I was then given it to examine in the witness box my mind went back to happier times, the Christmases filled with excitement and laughter. But now I was looking at the last picture of Vicky taken at Christmas. The last Christmas she ever had, I remember thinking. Then the tears came…

I'd managed to hold myself together for so long, but the emotion and the stress of giving evidence was taking its toll. I sipped some water and tried to compose myself again. I just felt so sad and alone in that court.

Frank finished his questioning and I felt relieved. I thought I'd answered well and got my points across clearly. I didn't know how long I'd been on my feet, but it seemed like hours. But now I would have to face another ordeal. I was about to be questioned by one of Scotland's toughest defence lawyers.

*

Donald Findlay is one of Scotland's most famous lawyers. He is renowned for taking on the most high-profile cases and has a reputation for being tough on witnesses. I must admit that I was concerned when I learned Donald Findlay was defending Tobin. If Tobin had any chance of eluding justice it would be because of the skills of his lawyer.

Findlay rose to his feet. He was such a recognisable figure with his dapper dress sense and his trademark whiskers. He looked like someone from a bygone age. His eyes were sharp and keen.

There were few niceties when he began his questioning, and within moments his manner had become more abrasive and his questioning more pointed.

'You didn't really have a close relationship with your sister, did you?' demanded Findlay.

I could feel the anger rising inside me. But that's what

he wanted, I thought. He wants me to react in front of the jury. I told myself I had to keep calm.

'We had a very good relationship,' I replied. 'We were close.'

Findlay then mentioned a name that rather confused me: a local eccentric who had befriended me and Vicky for a short while when I was 15 years old. At the time of Vicky's disappearance the police investigated him but found that he had a cast-iron alibi so I had put him to the back of my mind. I could only think that Findlay was trying to muddy the waters against Tobin by bringing him up now.

Findlay almost looked triumphant as he said he was in possession of a photograph of a girl posing on a bed with a whip. It was obvious by the way he was talking that the girl was Vicky. He suggested the picture had been taken by this man and he made comments to suggest that the photos were in some way incriminating.

I was shocked. I told him that I would have stopped anyone taking pictures of Vicky, especially this particular man.

I was very upset by this line of questioning. Why was he bringing up someone who had been fully investigated and discounted years ago? It looked like even at this early stage that the lawyer was trying to confuse the jurors and point the finger of blame for Vicky's murder at an alternative suspect.

Chapter Twelve

*

When I finished giving evidence it was like a huge weight had been lifted from my shoulders. As I walked from the witness box I felt like collapsing. The tension just drained from my body and I felt very weak.

However, I thought I'd done well, said the things I'd wanted to say and kept my composure. I'd managed to steal a few glances at the jury to try and gauge what kind of reaction they had to my evidence, but their faces gave little clue. The jury was made up of 12 women and three men – juries are 15-strong in Scotland compared to 12 in England and Wales – and I was surprised at the proportion of men to women. I'd have thought that Tobin's defence team might have objected to so many females on the jury, bearing in mind the case was about the murder of a young woman.

When I left the courtroom Brian was there to give me a big hug. I had prepared for my moment in the witness box for so long and I was just so glad I'd got through it. The fact I'd finished my evidence meant I could sit in the main courtroom for the remainder of the trial. As I had been one of the first prosecution witnesses I hadn't missed hearing a great deal of the evidence, and I was determined I would sit through the evidence of every single witness and would hear every detail of what happened to my little sister. I knew it was going to be difficult at times and that there was going to be a great deal of forensic evidence which I would find difficult to listen to. But I knew I had to do this. I had to know.

I was now legally allowed to catch up on what I had missed waiting in the court witness room, and I set about reading the reports from the first couple of days of the trial.

One of the first witnesses – a police photographer called Kenneth Fairley – told how he photographed a hunting-style knife found in the loft of the house Tobin used to live in at 11 Robertson Avenue in Bathgate. He said the double-edged six-inch blade was lying behind a floor joist and hard up against the house gable end.

The court was also told Vicky's purse was found among debris under a portable cabin which had been sited at Edinburgh's St Andrew's bus station. Inside were Vicky's hospital appointment card, an identity card, a bus ticket for 85p dated the day Vicky went missing and a shop receipt for toys, including a doll bought just before Christmas 1990.

Reading the reports, I could see how the prosecution was attempting to paint a picture to give the jury a step-by-step account of the day of Vicky's disappearance and the days leading up to it.

On Monday 10 November I was able to sit in the courtroom for the first time, my duties as a witness now at an end. I was worried about bumping into my father, but as he was still due to give evidence he was encamped in a local pub and wasn't allowed in open court.

I took a seat on the left-hand side of the public benches near the front and quite close to where the jury was seated. Brian was with me and Lee and his girlfriend were also there for support. I watched as Tobin was led into the court and was struck again by how small and wiry he appeared. Almost insignificant.

Looking at him I remember thinking back years ago that as he watched the police search the whole of the UK for Vicky, he must have thought he had got away with the perfect crime.

I had no idea what I would hear that day, but I had prepared myself mentally to accept that a lot of what would be said would be unpleasant. I was determined that Tobin would not drive me away. I didn't care if Tobin saw me crying, after all to cry is human, and he, in my eyes, was a monster.

The first few witnesses told of the night Vicky went missing, and in particular, the time she spent in Bathgate town centre before she was due to catch her connecting bus to Falkirk.

For the first time I learned there had been a couple of other sightings of Vicky that night – people who had never come forward before. A businessman called Robert Meechan said he was heading for a video store when a 'polite young lady' asked him for directions to the bus stop in South Bridge Street.

Also a retired driving instructor called Catherine Bryce said she was driving along South Bridge Street when a girl who looked like Vicky ran into the road, forcing her to brake hard. These were new witnesses, and it was strange, after nearly 17 years of poring over the details of Vicky's final journey, to hear new people give their accounts.

There was also evidence from Janice Gray, a housing officer with West Lothian Council, who told the court that Tobin had swapped his house in Robertson Avenue for one in Margate in Kent. This was the same house where Vicky's remains were found. This was damning evidence in my mind. Could it be just a coincidence that Tobin lived in Bathgate when Vicky went missing and then nearly 17 years later her body was found in the garden of a house he had moved to?

Tobin's QC had lodged a special defence of alibi before the case started. Tobin claimed he was not in Bathgate the night Vicky went missing but was in Portsmouth and did not arrive in Scotland until the following day. I was delighted when one of the early witnesses appeared to blow a hole in his claims.

Tobin's former next-door neighbour in Bathgate said that she caught a glimpse of him near a pub in the town on the night Vicky went missing. Wendy Love said she was certain of the date because she had been out in Bathgate that night celebrating a friend's 20th birthday.

At about half past ten or quarter to eleven she was standing outside a bar in the town centre when someone shouted from across the road.

'Somebody came to my attention,' she said.

'Who was that?' she was asked.

'Mr Tobin,' she replied.

I could have hugged her. I smiled over at her, willing her to be strong and she smiled back. Here was someone who placed Tobin in Bathgate on the night of Vicky's disappearance. Now his lawyer would have to provide witnesses to prove his claims that he was elsewhere on 10 February. It was a significant moment.

If that day was a good day the next was, by contrast, devastating.

I had to face the revelation that Vicky had gone to her doctor for a pregnancy test just a few weeks before she went missing.

Her doctor, Keith Orr, read from Vicky's medical record for November 1990: '? Pregnant. Spoke to nurse.' The doctor told the court that Vicky was not pregnant and nothing had been done to follow up her visit, even though her fears indicated under-age sex.

I was shattered. Vicky hadn't told me anything about

this. I knew she was interested in boys, but she had never confided in me that she was having sex. I realised that perhaps this fact would not play well in the eyes of the jury as Vicky was only fifteen when she had the test. I hoped it wasn't the only surprise in store.

If this evidence was difficult to hear, there was worse to follow the next day. The detailed evidence about where Vicky's body was found was outlined in court.

I'd been warned by Frank Mulholland that I might want to miss this evidence as he thought it might be upsetting for me. But I was determined to hear everything, no matter how graphic. The evidence was dramatic, and extremely upsetting.

The court was shown a computer simulation that reconstructed the excavation of female remains from Peter Tobin's old house in Margate. The footage showed how body parts were found buried in plastic bags in a grave in the back garden of the house.

In one package, wrapped in bin bags and a piece of cloth, was the lower torso of a female, placed upright in a kneeling position.

Beside it, in another package, an upper torso lay on its back with its hands together, almost covering the face. It had been wrapped in a blue curtain and a white cloth was sticking to the body.

The court was completely silent, transfixed by the

images before them on the screens around the room. Even although it was a computer image, it still seemed so real and lifelike. Was this how my sister ended up? Literally cut in half and dumped in a hole in the ground. It was horrific. Part of me wanted to leave the court, but I told myself I had to see it through.

I turned to where Tobin sat in the dock and stared at him with a look of total disgust. He caught my glare and turned to me and sneered. I just continued to stare at him until he looked away. This old man did not scare me.

I sat in a state of shock as scenes of crime officer Zoe Miller said the packages were removed from the garden grave on 12 November 2007 and a post-mortem examination was carried out the following day. She said a number of tissue samples were taken from the body and that ligatures were removed from both the upper and lower torso. It was like hearing the script for an X-rated horror movie, but the victim wasn't an actress, she was my own flesh and blood: my sister. It was one of the most harrowing days of the trial and I felt at an all-time low.

The next major piece of evidence outlined to me the wonders of modern science. The Home Office pathologist Dr David Rouse revealed that Vicky's body had been so well preserved after years entombed underground that he could tell that she may have been strangled – even after 17 years.

He said: 'There are no obvious signs of major blunt or sharp penetrating injury. Apparent bruising of the neck over the front of the spine may indicate death from neck compression.' However, he added that although Vicky's remains were well preserved, 'decomposition prevents precise determination of the cause of death.'

There was also evidence from Simon Nottle, who worked for Brighton Water Department between 1973 and 1977. He said Tobin had been part of the same maintenance gang as he was and would have known how to dig holes to a professional standard.

'The way the hole has been excavated is the way we would teach people to do it,' he said.

I was confident that the case was slowly but surely building up against Tobin. But there had to be a definite link between him and Vicky. At the moment it was all circumstantial.

Just when I thought I had heard all the harrowing details possible about Vicky's death, the next day's evidence was by far the most difficult to take in.

Evidence given by expert witness Professor Anthony Busuttil revealed that in his opinion Vicky desperately fought for her life after being drugged and pinned to the floor. I just wanted to cry through his entire evidence.

Poor Vicky. She must have gone through hell. I often thought when listening to his words that I was so glad

Mum wasn't alive to hear his graphic account of Vicky's last moments. She had been spared that, at least.

Busuttil told the court that bruising found on Vicky's right hand, chest, back and neck pointed to a violent struggle shortly before she died. He also confirmed something that was mentioned in the charges against Tobin which I'd read some months before. He said he believed Vicky may have been subjected to a serious sexual assault around the time of her death.

As he spoke to Professor Busuttil, Frank Mulholland outlined a scenario that described how Vicky might have died. He said: 'Vicky is on the floor. Someone has their knee or leg on her chest. Her neck is being compressed.

'She tries to defend herself, to stop this happening. Her right hand is free. The person who is doing this, when Vicky is trying to defend herself with her right hand, strikes her hand and continues to press her neck.

'Are these injuries and bruises consistent with the hypothesis I have put to you?'

'Yes,' said Professor Busuttil.

He also referred to toxicology tests that revealed that the drug amitryptiline had been found in Vicky's body. Peter Tobin had in the past been prescribed the drug, an anti-depressant, which can make the person who takes it drowsy.

This was hard to take. I couldn't believe the detail the doctors were able to glean from a post-mortem. It was just horrific hearing in graphic detail about what had happened to my sister.

I left the court to go back to my hotel feeling extremely sad and low. This was taking more out of me than I thought, and there were still two weeks of the trial to go.

After a reasonable sleep I was refreshed enough to face the ordeal of the next day's evidence. And at last a direct physical link between Tobin and Vicky emerged.

The court heard evidence from a fingerprint expert who revealed that Tobin's fingerprints were found on a black bag containing parts of Vicky's body when it was removed from the garden in Kent. James Aitken said he and a colleague found four clear matches for Tobin's prints on the refuse sack.

It was a eureka moment. How would Tobin explain his own prints on a bag containing Vicky's remains? Again, it was hard to hear, but it was worth going through this mental pain to get justice for Vicky.

It was now into the third week of the trial, and to my mind the evidence was growing stronger against Tobin. You can never be sure of the outcome of any criminal case, but I was quietly confident that the jury would convict this man. Every day I sat near to where the jury were, and sometimes one of them would smile at me as they went by to take their seats. I took it as a signal that they were on my side, but perhaps I was just over-sensitive to every little nuance.

Chapter Twelve

Throughout the evidence I kept glancing at the jury to see what their reaction was to what the witness was saying. Perhaps I was becoming paranoid. I was just so convinced Tobin was guilty. I could only hope that they were too.

*

Brian and I had been staying in a hotel in Dundee during the days the case was being heard, so it was a welcome relief going home for the weekend. Our friends had been a fantastic help looking after John and Emma-Jane, but I was so glad to see them when we got home on Friday nights. It was a case of getting back to normality after the tensions and pressures of sitting in the courtroom.

The following week – as it turned out, the final week of evidence – was the most dramatic and upsetting. We arrived back in Dundee, and after a short stop-off at the hotel, headed straight to the court.

The evidence we heard on Monday 24 November was the most damning so far against Tobin, and it also highlighted modern scientific developments in a most extraordinary way.

Forensics expert Nicola Clayson's evidence was compelling. She said she had examined Vicky's purse and found DNA on it that matched that of Tobin's son. She said it was probably traces of his saliva. For this to have happened Tobin must have given Vicky's purse to his son to play with or he simply picked it up from somewhere and put it in his mouth. It was damning evidence.

It also made me wonder if Tobin had his son in the car with him when he picked Vicky up that night in Bathgate. I could picture the scene. Vicky is waiting for her bus, Tobin pulls up and offers her a lift. She sees he has a young toddler in the back seat and thinks she is safe.

I couldn't help thinking that if Tobin had used his son as an unwitting accessory in picking up Vicky then he was even more despicable than I imagined.

The next day's continued evidence from Nicola Clayson was just as dramatic – and damning – as the evidence she gave the day before. And, again, her words were extremely hard to listen to.

She told the court that DNA tests on a tiny scrap of tissue stuck to the side of the knife found in attic of Tobin's old house in Bathgate concluded that it was Vicky's skin. She said the chances of the tissue belonging to anyone else rather than the schoolgirl were one in a billion.

I immediately looked at the jury. They all seemed transfixed by her words. If proof were needed that Tobin was Vicky's killer, then surely we had just heard it. It confirmed in my mind that Vicky was murdered in Bathgate and then transported down to Tobin's new home in Margate where he buried her.

But Nicola Clayson's next piece of evidence was

extremely hard for me to hear – even although it was mentioned in the charge against Tobin.

She said that tests on samples taken from Vicky's body suggested she may have been sexually assaulted by Tobin. She said two intimate swabs from Vicky had produced partial profiles that matched samples taken by police from Tobin. In one case she said the probability of the match coming from another man was one in 114. In the other case the figure was one in 34,000.

'In my opinion, it is most likely to have originated from semen,' she told the court.

No matter how much you try and prepare for hearing something like this, it is still difficult to deal with when the words are actually spoken. Not only had he murdered poor Vicky, Tobin had obviously forced himself on her before he did so. Words cannot describe the utter contempt I felt for Tobin as I sat in that court staring at him.

Throughout this sensitive evidence, Tobin never gave any clue as to what he was thinking. He would either stare at the ground or scribble notes on the pad in front of him in the dock. I just wanted him to react in some way, but no, there was nothing.

With this final damning evidence Frank Mulholland said he had completed the Crown's case against Tobin, and we all waited expectantly to see who Donald Findlay QC would call in defence of his client.

We needn't have worried.

Apart from one statement from a woman called Helen Maxwell from Bathgate, who claimed that she saw a girl similar to Vicky heading away from Bathgate town centre on 10 February 1991, there were no other significant witnesses.

I was astonished. Where was Tobin's alleged alibi that we had all been expecting to hear about? Why had Findlay not put Tobin himself in the witness box?

I knew he had been trying to muddy the waters when he mentioned a previous suspect, but why, then, had he not called *him* as a witness?

There was literally *no* case for the defence. How could any jury fail to convict Tobin after this debacle? All I could do now was hope and pray that the good members of the jury saw it the same way I did.

*

As I pulled back the curtains in my hotel room on the morning of Tuesday 2 December, I knew immediately that today was the day I would finally get justice for Vicky. It was snowing heavily – just like it was on the night I hugged and kissed her goodbye all those years ago. I felt the tears welling up as I watched the flakes fall softly to the ground. This had to be an omen. But was it a good one?

The judge was due to address the jury today, then they would retire to consider their verdict. Their verdict. A verdict at last after 17 years. I just had to pray it was the right one.

As I left the hotel with Brian it seemed my whole family had arrived in Dundee to support me on this final day. Of course, Lee and Lindsay were there, both just as anxious as me.

My dad and Christine were also there surrounded by their family, but I was determined not to let family differences get in the way.

I took my seat at the front of the court's public gallery on the left hand side near the jury and waited as they walked in to be addressed by the judge, Lord Emslie, on the various points of law. We listened intently as he emphasised the important role they had and told them that to return a guilty verdict against Tobin they would have to be satisfied 'beyond reasonable doubt' that he had killed Vicky. How could they be in any doubt? I thought as I listened to his speech.

In Scotland the jury also have two options to acquit: not guilty and the very controversial not proven verdict, a sort of 'no-man's land' verdict, that would leave Tobin's guilt or otherwise hanging in the air.

At precisely 12.20 p.m. on 2 December 2008, the jury of twelve women and three men retired to consider their verdict – and our waiting began. I felt sick to the pit of my stomach. This was it. We were now in the final hours of our 17-year wait.

I didn't know what I would do if the jury returned a verdict of not guilty. I hadn't really prepared for that. It had to be guilty. It had to be the right decision.

It seemed the world's press had gathered at court that day. There were hordes of photographers across the street and TV vans with huge satellite dishes lined up the road leading to the court.

The court officials had set aside a room for the immediate family members to use and I was grateful that I had somewhere warm to sit as it was sub-zero outside. But waiting in there, looking at the four bare walls, drove me mad. I found myself pacing the floor and popping outside occasionally for a breath of fresh air.

How long would the jury take? Would they come back with a verdict today or would they deliberate overnight? The suspense was unbelievable. All we could do was sit around and wait.

I had agreed with Lee and Lindsay that we would read a statement after the verdict to give our reaction and to thank the police. We also planned to mention the family of Polish student Angelika Kluk, who Tobin had been convicted of murdering in 2007. If it hadn't been for the police inquiry into her killing, detectives might never have made the link between Tobin and Bathgate.

Lindsay had agreed to read out the statement – a brave decision, as she would have to say these words in front of an army of journalists, some broadcasting to millions of people. I admired her for volunteering and marvelled that she felt strong enough to do it.

But at this moment none of us felt particularly strong. We were all too anxious. The jury had deliberated for half an hour before breaking for lunch at 1 p.m. and resuming at 2 p.m. It was now 3.30 p.m. and there was no sign of them returning with a verdict. This was hellish.

A court official told us that the judge would probably allow the jury to deliberate until 4.30 p.m. before calling them back to ask if they were anywhere near reaching a verdict. If they said yes he would give them a bit longer. If they said no he would send them home for the night before returning in the morning. I prayed this wouldn't happen. I couldn't stand another day of this unbearable tension.

Then, out of the blue, around 3.40 p.m. we heard a bell ring. Then a court official came into our room and said: 'They're coming back.' It took a couple of seconds for his words to sink in before we dashed towards the court door. Was this it, or were they coming back to ask a question on a point of law? Please, please let it be the verdict.

As I waited in court for the jury to take their seats the entire situation overwhelmed me and I burst into tears. I looked round and Lee and Lindsay were crying too. I suppose it was the enormity of it all. If this was the verdict then this was the end of the journey we had all shared for the last 17 years.

Then, suddenly the jury were walking into court. Lee, Lindsay and I all bowed our heads. We didn't want to look at them. I didn't want to try and read the expressions on their faces. I also didn't want the jury to have any pity for us. I could feel this was it. They weren't coming back to ask a question. This was it. It was the verdict.

Tobin was already in his seat in the dock flanked by two prison guards. He just stared straight ahead.

The court was completely silent as the clerk stood up and asked the foreman of the jury to stand. One of the three men on the jury rose to his feet.

'On the first charge, the charge of murder, have you reached a verdict,' he asked the foreman.

'Yes,' he replied.

I held my breath.

'What is your verdict?' he asked.

'Guilty.'

There was a concerted gasp of 'Yes' from the court-room and I just collapsed sobbing into Lee and Lindsay's arms. He was guilty. Guilty of my sister's murder.

The sound of the handcuffs snapping shut on Tobin's wrists was clearly heard above the noise from the public gallery.

'We did it,' whispered Lindsay as we quietly wept.

The clerk asked the foreman if they had reached their verdict by majority or unanimously. 'Unanimous,' came the reply.

Every member of the 15-strong jury had believed Tobin killed Vicky. There was absolutely no doubt in their mind.

My heart was thumping and I just couldn't stop crying. Brian was sitting in the row behind me and kept hugging me. There were tears in his eyes too. I wanted to shout out, not in joy, but in sheer relief, but I had to try and calm down.

I looked across to my right where Tobin was sitting, but I couldn't see him properly because of the security guard sitting next to him. I was desperate to fix his gaze.

Frank Mulholland addressed the court and read out Tobin's previous convictions and also informed the jury that he was currently serving a life sentence for Angelika Kluk's murder.

Then one of the officials ordered Tobin to stand. He was about to receive his sentence.

Lord Emslie stared at Tobin and began speaking to him: 'Abducting and killing a child on her way home from a happy weekend with her sister and then desecrating her body must rank among the most evil and horrific acts that any human being could commit.

'Once again you have shown yourself to be unfit to live in a decent society.

'This was a vulnerable teenager who needed help on her way home. But instead she fell into your clutches and you brought her short life to an end in a disgusting and degrading way.

'It is hard for me to convey the loathing and repulsion that ordinary people will feel for what you have done.'

Then he told Tobin he would have to serve 30 years in prison before he would be considered for parole. There was another gasp from the court. This was what I wanted to hear. It meant Tobin would be 92 before he could even be considered for release. Effectively it meant he would die in prison.

As Tobin was led away to the cells I just couldn't hold out any longer. As he turned to face me I shouted, 'Beast. Rot in hell,' at him. I just wanted to get back at him somehow. But he just kept walking with no emotion showing on his face. It looked for the world as if he was treating this as any other normal day.

The judge then thanked the jury for their time and for the way they had conducted themselves. I just felt like hugging each and every one of them. As they filed out of court I could see tears in some of their eyes and caught a couple of them smiling at me.

Then, spontaneously, the entire court began a round of applause as if thanking the jury for bringing back a guilty verdict. Not quite court protocol, but it did seem appropriate.

Chapter Twelve

As Lord Emslie left the court I was surrounded by my entire family hugging and kissing me and saying 'Well done.' My mind was a whirl. I couldn't believe it was over. Up until this point I'd never allowed myself to truly believe this day would come. Now it was reality, it was hard to take in.

I thought of Mum and how proud she would be that we had pursued Vicky's killers to the bitter end. She'd be smiling from up above, I thought. Justice at last for Vicky. We never gave up and today was our day.

After the tears and the horror of hearing what had happened to Vicky – details that no family should have to hear about one of their own – this was our time.

As I made my way out of court and looked at the blanket of snow on the ground my mind travelled back to the night I kissed Vicky goodbye 17 long years ago, my guilt at being the last member of her family to see her alive, and my helplessness as I realised something terrible had happened to her.

Now I felt so glad I'd never given up the fight to find Vicky. I couldn't. I owed her so much.

Epilogue

IN APRIL 2009 my little sister would have been 34 years old. In her 34 years who knows what she might have achieved.

She would probably have fallen in love, married and had children. Who knows how many nieces and nephews I would have enjoyed? And Vicky would have been a fantastic auntie to my kids, she loved children so much.

She was smart enough to have fulfilled her dream of becoming a vet. Her love of animals and in particular horses would have ensured she would have reached her goal.

In the weeks after the trial I visited her grave many times: when I needed strength, time to think, or just simply when I missed her. And miss her I do – desperately.

Over the previous 17 years I'd become accustomed to her being 'missing'; to her being intangible. But she was home now. She had been put to rest at last by the people who loved her.

My sister was more than the girl in a school photograph,

more than the face on a missing poster. She was a kind, generous and beautiful person, who I long for every day. I miss the girl she was and the woman she could have been.

She was robbed of her life just as she was beginning to savour the very essence of it. I was robbed of Vicky, the most wonderful sister in the world.

And yet I still feel her presence now, looking after me and my family. Her spirit lives on and I know she is smiling down at me.

She is back with me now, and nothing will separate us ever again.

Acknowledgements

This book was inspired by my siblings Vicky, Lee and Lindsay, and also my children, John and Emma-Jane.

Vicky had lots of friends, many of whom have been in touch to show their support. Vicky would have been so proud of you all. I would like to say a special thank you to Linzi Baird who helped give Vicky a lot of special times while they were young girls. I'd also like to thank her for allowing me to use her precious photographs.

Thanks to Liz and John Crozier, Brian's parents, for without him I would be a wandering soul. I love him dearly, for the love and support he has blessed me with. Thank you, Brian. To Ian, Elinor and Susan Miller, and to John and Sandra Hamilton, who helped so much over the years, and the rest of our extended family. Thanks to Angela Sneddon, Karen Booth and Brian and Gayle Mungal for all their support and friendship.

I owe a great deal of thanks to Frank Mulholland for securing the conviction and also to his colleagues and staff who supported my family before and during the trial. I would like to thank Shona Livingston who helped our mother at a time of need, also her colleagues at West Lothian and Borders Police and Central Scotland Police, who all tried, in vain, to find Vicky. We are eternally grateful to DCI Keith Anderson for never giving up and for finally finding Vicky. Thank you to Alan Crow, Random House and Vermilion for helping me to keep Vicky's memory alive.

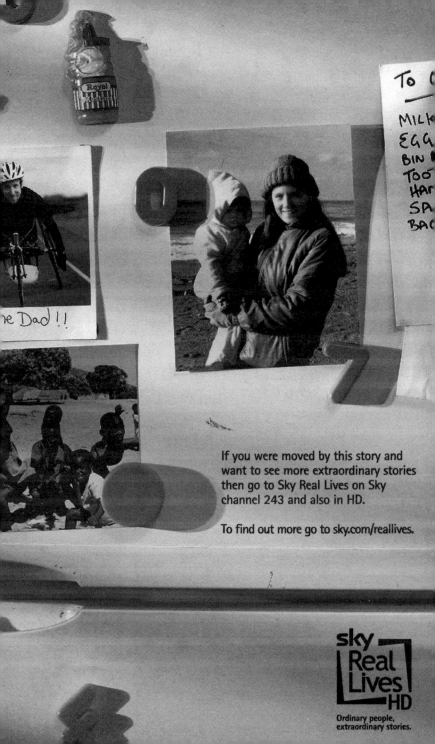